Walking Eye
mobile app

Discover the world's best destinations with the Insight Guides Walking Eye app, available to download for free in the App Store and Google Play.

The container app provides easy access to fantastic free content on events and activities taking place in your current location or chosen destination, with the possibility of booking, as well as the regularly-updated Insight Guides travel blog: Inspire Me. In addition, you can purchase curated, premium destination guides through the app, which feature local highlights, hotel, bar, restaurant and shopping listings, an A to Z of practical information and more. Or purchase and download Insight Guides eBooks straight to your device.

Available on the **App Store**

Get it on **Google play**

KV-511-383

INSIGHT GUIDES

Walking Eye

- DESTINATIONS
- INSPIRE ME
- EBOOKS
- EVENTS

TOP 10 ATTRACTIONS

DIVING
Discover the wonders of the deep at numerous dive sites around the islands. See page 85.

HIKING
The cool mountains of Morne Seychellois National Park are great for walks. See page 43.

CYCLE AROUND LA DIGUE
One great way to explore laid-back La Digue is by bicycle. See page 58.

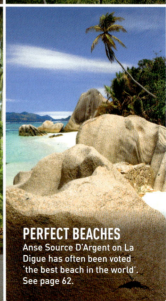

PERFECT BEACHES
Anse Source D'Argent on La Digue has often been voted 'the best beach in the world'. See page 62.

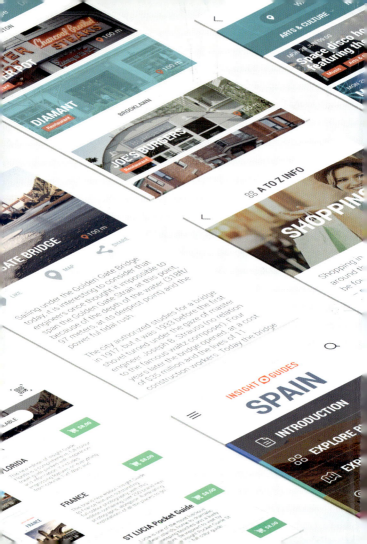

EXOTIC FLORA
Pitcher plants are among the islands' diverse botanic delights. See page 45.

VALLÉE DE MAI
This forest on Praslin is a must for coco de mer, walking trails and wildlife. See page 50.

BIRD ISLAND
Simple comforts are offered on this idyllic island. See page 77.

VICTORIA
Visit the capital for a taste of urban life and an insight into local history and culture. See page 25.

SAILING
The Seychelles was made for sailing, hire a boat or hop on a chartered tour to see the best of the islands. See page 90.

HAWKSBILL TURTLES
See these great creatures on Cousin from October to April. See page 68.

A PERFECT DAY

9am

Morning Market

In the morning visit the Sir Selwyn-Clarke Market, also known as Victoria Market, where stalls are piled high with freshly caught fish, neat pyramids of exotic fruits and seasonal vegetables. You'll also find trays of mixed spices, neatly rolled quills of fresh cinnamon, packets of turmeric and colourful jars filled with chillies.

12.30pm

Lunch and Art

Take a break at George Camille Art Gallery (Kaz Zanana) at Revolution Avenue where you can have a light lunch followed by the best chocolate cake and cappuccino you'll come across in the Seychelles. Afterwards, pop into the mini art gallery featuring works of local artist, George Camille.

10.30am

Central Victoria

Victoria is easy to explore. Begin your tour at the Clock Tower. Built in 1903 as a memorial to Queen Victoria and to commemorate the establishment of the Seychelles as a Crown Colony in its own right, the Clock Tower lies at a central crossroads in the centre of town. East of the Clock Tower is the Natural History Museum where you can see endemic birds, reef life, tortoises, geology and the skulls of estuarine crocodiles that once inhabited the mangrove swamps along Mahé's coast and terrorised the colonists.

1.30pm

Local Crafts

Codevar Craft Centre at Camion Hall in Albert Street is one of the best places to pick up gifts and souvenirs. In the arcade Kreol Or there is a wide range of jewellery made out of green snail shell, tiger cowrie, coconut shell and gold, and crafts made from local woods, coconut shell, coconut wood and polished palm seed.

5pm

Historic Roots

On the outskirts of Victoria is Bel Air cemetery, Seychelles' oldest cemetery. Settlers and their slaves are buried here from the earliest times. The more splendid tombs bear the names of illustrious Seychelles families. Tombstones lie strewn haphazardly, there are no signposts and no guide, but it is an atmospheric place, nonetheless.

7pm

Dinner

Move on for dinner at Marie-Antoinette at Serret Road, off the road to Beau Vallon, at the foot of Signal Hill above Victoria. The restaurant is apparently unchanged since the 1970s and is located in a beautiful, wood-and-iron colonial Seychellois mansion. They serve a set Creole menu of the day regularly featuring grilled fish and aubergine fritters, chicken curry, fish stew and rice and salad. The dessert menu is less imaginative, but by then you'll most likely be full anyway.

3pm

Natural Attractions

Visit the Botanical Gardens at the foot of Mount Fleuri. Look out for the elephant apple plants, which bear edible fruit such as huge apples that smell of rubber. A number of Aldabra giant tortoises are kept here in a large pen shaded by a coco de mer palm. There are attractive ponds with water lilies and darting dragonflies. The path leading from the ponds takes you past a mighty banyan tree and several drumstick trees that shed remarkable, long, thin fruit.

CONTENTS

INTRODUCTION

There are many tropical paradise islands, but none quite like the Seychelles. The main islands are the world's only mid-ocean granite outcrops. They are also the oldest ocean islands but have had a shorter period of human occupation than practically anywhere. You will never forget your first approach to Mahé, towering up out of the sapphire and cerulean seas, the majestic mountains swathed as though in green velvet, the spectacular totems of massive granite outcrops and boulders scattered amidst the dark emerald forest like Henry Moore sculptures. Houses cling to the lower slopes, but above a certain height there is nothing but forest. Each island has an atmosphere completely its own, and as a rule of thumb, for each decrease in size you travel back in time about ten years. Mahé is reminiscent of the late 1990s, Praslin the 1980s, La Digue the 1970s and beyond that the tiny islands are seemingly untouched by the

Giant tortoise (Geochelone gigantea) on Curieuse Island

hands of time. The Seychelles is one of the few places on earth where you can still experience the beauty of the natural world before mankind and mass tourism moved in. Make the most of having a beach or even a whole island to yourself and leave the woes of modern life behind.

Anse Cocos beach

More than 40 percent of the landmass of the Seychelles is included in National Parks (like the Morne, above), Special Reserves or other protected areas. Marine National Parks occupy a further 35 sq km (13.5 sq miles).

GEOGRAPHY AND CLIMATE

The Seychelles lies in the western Indian Ocean between approximately 4°S and 10°S and 46°E and 54°E. The number of islands listed in the Constitution is 155, the majority of which are small and uninhabited. The landmass is only 457 sq km (176 sq miles), but the islands are spread over an Exclusive Economic Zone of 1,374,000 sq km (530,000 sq miles). About 90 percent of the population of 90,000 live on Mahé, with just 9 percent on Praslin and La Digue. Around a third of the land area is the island of Mahé and a further third the atoll of Aldabra.

There are two distinct regions, the granite islands (the world's only oceanic islands formed of granite) and the coral-line outer islands. The granite islands are the world's oldest ocean islands, while the outer islands are mainly very young. The Aldabra group and St Pierre (Farquhar Group) are unusual, raised coral islands that have emerged and submerged several times during their long history - the most recent submergence dating from about 125,000 years ago.

The Seychelles climate is hot and humid all year around. The relatively dry southeast monsoon blows from May to October and the northwest monsoon from November to April, with calm periods in between. During the northwest monsoon,

A warm welcome at Praslin Airport

temperatures and humidity are higher, and though heavy downpours can occur year round, they are especially common mid-December to mid-February.

FLORA AND FAUNA

As a result of their antiquity, evolution has produced a rich endemic flora and fauna in the granitics, with 11 endemic bird species and about 80 species of plant. Many of these have their nearest relatives in Asia, despite the relative proximity of Africa. They include some of the rarest flora and fauna on earth, though thanks to strenuous conservation efforts, most of the birds and many plants are increasing in numbers, reversing the previous two centuries of decline. The outer islands have less endemic wildlife, except for Aldabra, but many islands have spectacular seabird colonies. Aldabra has everything from flightless birds to the world's biggest giant tortoise population.

PEOPLE AND LANGUAGE

The Seychelles was uninhabited until the second half of the 18th century. The Seychellois are a mélange of peoples, descended partly from the original French settlers and their slaves from Madagascar and Africa, then later Chinese labourers and Indian merchants. Despite the years as a British colony, few British settled here, though there was a subtle

British influence on Seychellois society. The greatest change in Seychelles society came with the mass influx of 'liberated Africans' in the 19th century, which altered the nature of the population, although one wonderful aspect of Seychelles society is the ease with which different races mix and live together.

The first plantation owners and their slaves devised a simplified form of French for communications. This has developed into modern Creole, a lively language that happily absorbs new phrases and vocabulary, especially from English. Some of the so-called *grand blan* descendants of the French, retain French as the language of the home, but will also speak Creole and English as necessary. Most Seychellois are trilingual. Creole has a simple grammar and is relatively easy to learn, although it can be difficult to understand when spoken quickly. Although a token effort at a few words in Creole is appreciated, it is easy to get by in English and most Seychellois are fluent in English and French.

Seychellois tend to look to Europe for their influences rather than to India or Africa. While many younger Seychellois live the sort of life familiar to anyone from the West, there are still those, particularly on the outer islands, who live life the old way, taking everything they need from the land and the sea. Everywhere, the attitude to life is reasonably relaxed and the Seychellois concept of time-keeping is often vague.

TOURISM AND ECONOMY

Tourism has been the biggest employer in the Seychelles since its international airport opened in 1971. This is not a destination for intense activity, the Seychelles is for those who really want to relax and get away from it all in the most beautiful and unspoilt conditions. You do not have to be a beach addict to appreciate and enjoy the islands – it is the atmosphere of 'other-worldliness' here that seduces most visitors.

Extreme conditions

When the tsunami of December 2004 swept across the Indian Ocean in its wave of mass destruction, the Seychelles was very fortunate. The full force of the tsunami struck at almost exactly low spring tide, and although some hotels, homes and bridges were badly damaged, only three lives were lost.

There are land-based activities such as golfing on Mahé or Praslin. Although the Seychelles is almost on the equator and the heat and humidity saps the energy, exploring the islands on foot is extremely rewarding, and a tour of La Digue by bicycle will charm you. Photographers and artists will be spoilt for choice, while naturalists and birdwatchers will see some of the rarest specimens on the planet.

The diving is excellent, the reefs free of crowds and pollution. Snorkelling is easy and all the usual watersports are available. The Seychelles is also a superb place to sail. The weather is relatively predictable, the waters around the inner islands are sheltered, and the close proximity of the islands means you can visit a different one every day.

THE PRICE OF EXCLUSIVITY

The beaches have few or no facilities, but this is part of the charm. You'll find no high-rise hotels or strings of restaurants along the beachfront – here it's just trees for shade and boulders to drape your towel on to dry. This exclusivity is part of the attraction but it comes at a price – this is no budget destination.

Tourism is the lynchpin of the economy. Before this, *copra* (dried coconut) was king, with cinnamon and vanilla alternately rising to prominence. Coconuts are dominant on every shoreline and cinnamon is still commonplace in the mountains. Fishing still has its place and ecotourism is high on the agenda to ensure the Seychelles remains a pristine tropical paradise.

A BRIEF HISTORY

It is still unknown as to who were the first peoples to set foot in the Seychelles. The dependability of the two annual monsoon winds meant that the Indian Ocean was one of the earliest oceans navigated regularly by the nations surrounding it: the Arabs, Chinese, Indians and Africans. We may be reasonably certain that Arab traders knew of the islands and called in occasionally. Portuguese navigator Jean de Nova came across the southern atolls of the Seychelles in 1501, and in 1505 Vasco da Gama sailed through and named the Amirantes. The Portuguese did not settle the islands, and neither did the next recorded visitors, the British. A storm-tossed vessel of the East India Company anchored off Mahé in January 1609. Impressed as they were by the beauty and natural bounties of the island, they found them deserted and did not remain long. The islands were left in obscurity for

A tapestry of an Arab boat navigating the Indian Ocean

a further 130 years, although they were probably used by pirates as hideaways.

BRITISH-FRENCH RIVALRY

It was Franco-British rivalry in India that brought an end to the Seychelles' isolation. British ships en route to India could break the long journey at the Cape, and the French needed a similar stopover. They had a base at Bourbon (Reunion) but there was no safe harbour there. There was an excellent sheltered bay at Port Louis on Isle de France (Mauritius) and the French claimed this island in 1721. They were therefore dismayed when there were rumours of British interest in the islands to their north, too close for comfort. Since little was known about the Seychelles (still without an official name) they sent an expedition from Mauritius to explore the islands, led by the sea captain Lazare Picault. He visited in 1742 and 1744, naming the largest granite island Mahé in honour of the French governor of Mauritius. The islands were not claimed formally by the French until 1756 when Captain Nicolas Morphey laid a stone of possession carved with the arms of France near to the site of modern Victoria. The island group was given the name of Séchelles, honouring a French minister.

In August 1770 the first settlers took up residence on

Prison Island

For the French and British, the Seychelles made an ideal prison. In 1810, over 70 'terrorists', accused of committing terrible crimes during the French Revolution, were exiled here for life. Many were later sent on to Anjouan (Comoros); those remaining settled down peaceably. The British sent troublesome leaders from other colonies to exile here, including the ex-Sultan of Perak (1875–95), ex-King Prempeh of Ashanti (1900–23), and Archbishop Makarios of Cyprus in the 1950s.

'A Fleet of East Indiamen at Sea', by Nicholas Pocock (1741–1821)

St Anne, an island opposite Port Victoria. There were 26 in the group of pioneers, including Frenchmen, Indians and slaves from Africa and Madagascar. This settlement was undertaken as a speculative venture by a private entrepreneur. He had official support but no financial backing. Soon afterwards a royal settlement was created on Mahé, at Anse Royale, where a garden was established in which precious spice plants, cinnamon, nutmeg and pepper were cultivated. The St Anne settlement ran out of money and discipline broke down. The settlers refused to work the land and moved to Mahé, where they made easy money selling tortoises and turtles (for meat) and timber to visiting ships. Alarmed by the devastation this caused in the islands, the French government took action, evacuating settlers who wanted to go home whilst a garrison of 15 soldiers kept order among those who remained, settling in the area of Victoria, known then as L'Etablissement.

The tiny French colony grew slowly, largely isolated from the turmoil of world events, until once again the battle for dominance in India between Britain and France altered the course of the Seychelles' history. The British captured Mauritius in 1812, and the Seychelles was considered by them to be included in the same package. The greatest change for the settlers came when the British took the first steps towards abolishing slavery in their colonies. Many planters abandoned the Seychelles, finding it impossible to farm effectively without free labour. One way around the problem was to plant coconut palms. There was a good market for coconut oil and copra and the trees needed relatively

THE LIBERATED AFRICANS

Having agreed to abolish slavery in its territories under the Emancipation Act of 1835, Britain set about enforcing the new law. This was deeply unpopular in some places, including the Seychelles, despite the fact that slavery was to be phased out gradually with ex-slaves becoming 'apprentices' for six years before they had absolute freedom, and former owners received compensation. By the 1860s, Britain had taken on a proactive role, attempting to suppress the slave trade worldwide. The Royal Navy operated anti-slavery patrols off the east African coast and elsewhere, in an effort to control the human traffic between Africa and the Gulf. Slave-trading dhows were pursued and boarded, the victims freed. These 'liberated Africans' were not returned to Africa in case they were immediately recaptured. Those from ships taken south of the equator were brought to the Seychelles where as many as could be employed were allowed to remain as 'apprentices'. Most adults worked on the coconut plantations or as domestic servants, whilst the children were given a basic education and taught a trade. In all, between 1861 and 1874 over 2,000 of these 'liberated Africans' were settled in the Seychelles.

little tending in comparison to the crops formerly grown, such as coffee and maize. In other respects the change in administrative power made little difference to the Seychellois whose language and customs were largely respected by the new government. Even the little capital was not given an English name until 1841 when it was renamed after Queen Victoria.

'View of Mahe' by Himely (1801-1872)

VANILLA AND COCONUTS

The population remained very small, with just a handful of French and British settlers, freed slaves of African and Madagascan origin and a few Indian families, and so the sudden arrival of almost 3,000 so-called 'liberated Africans' in the 1860s had a massive impact on the islands. With more labour available, more coconut plantations were established, some on the remoter coralline islands where there had formerly been no regular settlement. Other farmers turned to vanilla cultivation, which for a time was immensely lucrative and made some landowners very rich.

Just as Victoria was becoming established as a true island capital, a terrible storm caused the lower slopes of the mountain behind to slip away, burying much of the town in mud. At least 70 people were killed, buried alive or swept out to sea. Some areas of the present town are built upon the land thus created; 'reclaimed' by the mud from the sea. The colony recovered from this setback and prosperity increased as the 19th

Fishermen landing their catch in the early 1970s

century drew to a close. The Seychellois had begun to resent the fact that ultimately they were still administered by the British authorities in Mauritius, and so there was widespread celebration when the Seychelles finally became an independent Crown Colony in 1903, able to make many decisions about the islands' future for themselves, although they were still dependent on London for finance and no major project could be undertaken without the approval of the colonial government.

WORLD WARS TO INDEPENDENCE

The outbreak of war in 1914 was disastrous for the Seychelles. Largely cut off from shipping, exports were severely curtailed and grievous poverty ensued, despite the introduction of new cash crops such as cinnamon oil and guano. During the inter-war years it became clear that the Seychelles economy was in trouble, and World War II compounded the difficulties. The privations which resulted led to the formation of the first political party, the Association of Seychelles Taxpayers.

Although their members were mostly well-to-do, they also represented the less affluent in discussions with the ruling colonial power. In 1964 the Democratic Party (DP), led by James Mancham, and the Seychelles Peoples United Party (SPUP), led by France-Albert Rene, were created. Mancham wanted the colony to remain British, whilst Rene's socialist party advocated independence. Three years later, universal adult suffrage was introduced for elections to a Legislative Council which in 1970 became a Legislative Assembly. The DP won six seats in the elections and the SPUP five: Mancham was therefore made Chief Minister. From 1970 discussions were held with the British, who were shedding their colonies worldwide, about the future of the Seychelles, and it became independent in 1976. By the 1970s it had become clear that the best hope for the country's economic future lay in tourism, and this was progressed by a 'parting gift' from Britain of an international airport.

INDEPENDENCE AND THE MODERN ERA

Upon independence, the rival political parties agreed to a coalition between the DP and the SPUP, with Mancham as President and Rene as Prime Minister. However, on 5 June 1977, whilst Mancham was overseas on Government business, a coup d'état took place in which Rene took power. Opposition political parties were outlawed and new elections were called in 1979 with Rene as the sole candidate. Predictably, an overwhelming victory was

Governor police inspection in 1972

President James Alix Michel

claimed and a one-party socialist state was established, the SPUP becoming the Seychelles People's Progressive Front (SPPF).

During the Cold War, Rene successfully used the Seychelles' strategic importance to play America and the Soviet Union off against one other, obtaining substantial help from both superpowers. Whispers of a counter coup plot proliferated, and curfews were declared on several occasions. In 1981 a force of mercenaries attempted to take over the islands but they were discovered at the airport. They briefly took over the airport, but hijacked an Air India flight and fled to South Africa. A year later, mutineers in the Seychelles Army, maintaining loyalty to Rene but in revolt against conditions, took over Victoria. They were overcome by Tanzanian troops, whose intervention was requested by Rene.

With the end of the Cold War, pressure for reform increased. Rene initially opposed moves but in 1992 embraced multi-party democracy. Mancham returned but faced a different Seychelles. New opposition parties emerged, then coalesced to form the Seychelles National Party (SNP). Rene and the SPPF won elections held in 1993 and 1998. Opposition parties complained of intimidation and the uneven playing field caused by SPPF's control of the Government media and resources. In 2004 Rene passed the mantle of Presidency to his Vice President and faithful stalwart, James Michel.

HISTORICAL LANDMARKS

1609 First recorded landing, by an English East India Company ship.

Late 17th century Pirates probably using the Seychelles as a base.

1742–4 Frenchman Lazare Picault explores the Seychelles.

1756 French send expedition from Mauritius to claim Mahé.

1770 First French settlement created on St Anne Island.

1778 A French garrison stationed at *L'Etablissement* on Mahé.

1786 Population 151 (24 soldiers, five civilians and 122 slaves).

1812 Mauritius falls to British, together with the Seychelles.

1835 Abolition of slavery.

1840 First coconut plantations are established.

1841 *L'Etablissement* renamed Victoria.

1861 Arrival of first of 2,500 liberated Africans boosts population.

1891 Vanilla becomes an important cash crop.

1903 The Seychelles becomes an independent Crown Colony.

1914–18 Great hardship in the Seychelles due to isolation.

1926 Electricity and telephone services installed.

1939–45 The islands act as a refuelling base for warships.

1963 Construction of American satellite-tracking station on Mahé.

1964 Creation of SPUP and SDP, the first political parties.

1970 First Constitutional Conference on the future of Seychelles.

1971 International Airport opens and regular flights commence.

1976 The Seychelles is declared an independent republic. A coalition government of Mancham (President) and Rene (PM) is formed.

1977 Mancham overthrown in a coup establishing Rene as President.

1979 The Seychelles becomes a one-party Socialist State.

1981 Mercenary force fails to seize control of the country.

1992 Multi-party political system re-established. Mancham returns.

1993 Rene wins the election. New constitution is adopted.

2004 Rene steps down, passing Presidency to James Michel. The Seychelles is hit by the tsunami.

2009 The Seychelles and the EU sign an anti-piracy agreement.

2015 US$30 million buyback agreement to transfer debt to a conservation trust and the creation of an Indian Ocean marine reserve.

WHERE TO GO

Life in the Seychelles can be a beach. There is no finer place to relax and enjoy the sun, sand and sea, and few destinations give visitors such a feeling of escape. As well as some of the most beautiful beaches on earth, the Seychelles also offers visitors the chance to discover nature at its best between its rich marine life and majestic mountain forests. Most visits begin on Mahé.

MAHÉ

Mahé is the largest and highest island in the Seychelles, covering an area of 15,793 hectares (61 sq miles) and rising to 905m (2,970ft) above sea level. The island is 27km (17 miles) long and at its widest is 8km (5 miles) across. About 90 percent of the population lives on Mahé, concentrated in the north around Victoria and on the flat reclaimed land of the east coast. Away from the bustling capital and hotel beaches there is still extraordinary peace and beauty to be found along the coast and in the grandeur of the mountains.

VICTORIA

Victoria, the capital and only town of any size in the Seychelles, is situated on the east coast of Mahé. It was founded on this spot by the French in 1778 as L'Etablissement, because of its excellent natural harbour with shelter provided by St Anne and neighbouring islands. It gained its present name in 1841 in honour of the British queen. In modern times it has been extended seawards on reclaimed land where modern office blocks replace the colonial-style architecture of old Victoria.

The **Clock Tower** is the centre, the most striking landmark and the very symbol of Victoria. It is a replica of a clock tower

Anse Source d'Argent, La Digue

near Victoria Station in London (not of Big Ben, as is sometimes supposed). It was erected as a memorial to Queen Victoria, who died in 1901, but as it took until 1903 to get it to the Seychelles, it also marks the year that the Seychelles became a Crown Colony independent of Mauritius. This is the best place from which to navigate your way around the capital. Legend has it that this clock chimes the hour twice, better to stir the laid-back population into action. In fact the clock arrived in kit form, and in a mishap during unloading, the pendulum was dropped over the side of the ship, and, despite a makeshift substitute being made locally, the chime was disabled. The clock at the Catholic Cathedral does chime twice, however, once before and once after the hour.

Parallel to the coast, **Albert Street** leads north towards Beau Vallon and **Francis Rachel Street** south towards the airport. This was once the waterfront, and many of the quaint old buildings still survive here, squeezed between less charismatic modern offices and shops. **State House Avenue** leads inland to the gates of State House, the President's office. This is a beautiful colonial-style building, sadly not open to the public. In the grounds is the tomb of Queau de Quincy, the most successful of the French administrators of the islands who steered the young colony through some very difficult times during the wars between England and France. In the opposite direction, **Independence Avenue** leads towards the sea.

On the corner of Independence Avenue and Francis Rachel Street is the Law

Reclaimed land

Most of Victoria east of the Clock Tower and south to the airport, plus the islands between St Anne and Mahé, were reclaimed by dredging dead coral from the surrounding sea bed. Such land has also been used for the airport, housing and industrial sites.

The Clock Tower

Courts, an attractive well-maintained colonial-style building. Beneath the shady trees in the grounds of the building is a water fountain, topped with a tiny replica **statue of Queen Victoria**. The original, now held in the History Museum, was unveiled in 1900 to mark the 60th year of the Queen's reign. Another historical monument faces the mountains, a **bust of Pierre Poivre**, the governor of Mauritius who founded a spice garden in the Seychelles.

The **History Museum** (open Mon–Tues and Thur–Fri 8.30am–4.30pm, Wed 8.30am-noon, Sat 9am–1pm; charge) is situated in the National Library Building on Francis Rachel Street. In the entrance is the **Stone of Possession**, a stone placed by the French in 1756 to claim the islands. Displays are very simple without any interactive or animated exhibits, but for those interested in the history of the islands it is an excellent introduction. The peaceful air-conditioned hall is also a pleasant, cool retreat from the heat and bustle of the capital.

There is a small art gallery on the opposite side of the museum car park, **Carrefour des Arts** (open Mon–Fri 9am–5pm; free), with original paintings on sale. Whether or not you are an art lover, it is well worth taking the time to visit **Kenwyn House ❶** (open Mon–Fri 8am–4pm, Sat 9am–noon; free), directly opposite the main entrance to the National Library on Francis Rachel Street. This is one of the best-preserved 19th-century buildings in Victoria. Apart from the architecture, it contains a fairly extensive art gallery featuring many local artists.

LOCAL MAGIC

The origins of *grigri*, the local magic, are obscure, but probably lie in Africa and Madagascar. Its uses are in the main positive: a love potion perhaps, or protection from the evil intent of others, for which you must go to a *bonnonm* or *bonnfanm dibwa* (respectively, a male or female sorcerer). The tools of the trade are a motley collection of everyday items: playing cards, tea leaves, small stones and mirrors with which they read the future, diagnose your illness or discern who wishes you ill. Some are also healers, who know how to use the local plants medicinally, but you might come away with a little packet containing chips of wood and sawdust to boil to make a medicine, or some mystery powder, incense and wood to burn, the ashes to be buried near the doorstep whilst you state aloud what you want the spell to achieve.

Some *bonnonms* became legendary, including Charles Dialor to whom conventional doctors were said to recommend patients when they were baffled. There were attempts to suppress *grigri* in the 1950s, but although most Seychellois these days just go to the doctor when they are ill, some belief in the power of the *bonnonm* still lingers.

The **Natural History Museum** (open Mon–Fri 8.30am–4.30pm, Sat 8.30am–noon, closed Sun; charge) is situated on Independence Avenue near to the Post Office. This is well worth a visit even if you have little interest in the subject, telling as it does something of the story of the Seychelles. There are displays of indigenous birds, marine life, tortoises, geology and extinct species. Exhibitions are held upstairs and permanent displays include copies of the famous paintings of Marianne North, a British artist who visited the Seychelles from 1883 to 1884.

Kenwyn House

On the opposite side of the road is Victoria's most popular restaurant, the **Pirates Arms**. This relaxed café-bar opens onto the street, so there is never a shortage of subjects for discussion. It's open all day and into the evening for a meal, snack or drink. There is a small arcade of shops beside it, several of which sell curios.

Independence Avenue terminates at a roundabout featuring the Bicentennial Monument known as Trwa Zwazo (three birds), erected in 1978 to celebrate 200 years of human settlement in the Seychelles. Each 'bird' represents one of the continents in the blood of the Seychellois: Europe, Africa and Asia. Continuing straight on, the road leads to the **Inter-Island Quay**, the departure point for charter boats and ferries to Praslin.

From the *Trwa Zwazo* Roundabout, 5th June Avenue heads south to **Marine Charter Association**. This departure point for glass-bottom boats and some charter yachts is 150m (165yds) along the southern section of the road. Almost opposite is the statue *Zonm Lib* (free man), supposed to symbolise the liberation of the Seychellois after the 1977 coup d'état, which ushered in 16 years of one-party rule.

Returning once more to the clock tower, nearby on the corner of Albert Street and Revolution Avenue stands **St Paul's Anglican Cathedral**. This was the Seychelles' oldest church, consecrated in 1859, but little of the original structure remains. A little further along on the opposite side of the road is **Camion Hall**, which houses small souvenir shops. Further along again, Albert Street joins with Market Street, which runs inland parallel to Revolution Avenue. This is a pedestrianised zone, except for vehicles delivering produce

Trading at Sir Selwyn Selwyn-Clarke Market

to the **Sir Selwyn Selwyn-Clarke Market**, named in honour of a former governor. The money to build this market had to be raised by public subscription, the authorities in Mauritius being unwilling to pay for it. The street is always crowded during working hours, but particularly on Saturday mornings when the Seychellois buy their fresh fish, essential for the weekend.

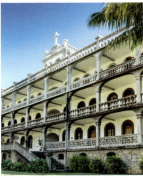

Grand Capuchin House

Church Street leads from Market Street to the **Roman Catholic Cathedral**. Again, little remains of the original building dating from 1874, having been rebuilt in granite in 1933. One of Victoria's most impressive buildings, the Catholic Priests' Residence, **Capuchin House** is beside the cathedral. The alleyway adjacent to the market is Benezet Street, leading back to Revolution Avenue, emerging opposite Central Police Station.

THE BOTANICAL GARDENS

On the southern edge of Victoria, the **Botanical Gardens** ❷ (open daily 8am–5pm; charge) provide a gentle contrast with the capital. The best time to visit is early in the morning, the middle of the day being too hot for walking. The late afternoon is also good, though some blooms will have faded by this time. There are no refreshments on sale in the gardens and it is a good idea to take a bottle of water with you. There is a car park by the entrance and a small kiosk, where the entrance fee is paid and a leaflet is provided, which includes a plan of the gardens and names of many of the most interesting plants. From here, the tarmac path leads uphill, but you are free to wander as you please.

The 6-hectare (15-acre) site was laid out in 1901 by Rivaltz Dupont, a French botanist, who also collected many of the plant specimens during his travels. He converted a tangled undergrowth between two babbling streams into the cool, peaceful atmosphere visitors can experience today. The main path is lined with exotic and endemic palms. To the left, lawns incline towards the river.

After about 100m (165yds) from the car park there is a turning to the right and on the opposite corner there is a mature coco de mer tree and a large pen containing Aldabra giant tortoises. Continuing uphill, the gardens open out on the right, the broad lawn dotted with exotic trees and shrubs. Beyond this there is an attractive pond with water lilies and darting dragonflies. The path leads uphill to the top of the gardens. Giant fruit bats may be seen roosting in the trees towards the mountains and blue pigeons flit by.

The path now turns left downhill past the roots of an impressive banyan tree and several cannonball trees, with their strange, fleshy red flowers. At the bottom of the bank turn right to return to the car park.

Beau Vallon beach

BEAU VALLON

Northwest of Victoria, **Beau Vallon** ❸ is the most popular beach in the Seychelles, with three large hotels and several smaller establishments in the vicinity. Nevertheless, it is only really busy at weekends when locals join tourists to enjoy the beach and watersports.

Two of the best dive centres in the Seychelles are situated at Coral Strand Hotel and Beau Vallon Bay Hotel. Paragliding is also popular. Other activities include the usual range of watersports from windsurfing to water skiing and banana boat rides.

Creole doll at the Craft Village

Beau Vallon is an excellent beach for swimming and safe for children, with soft sand, no undertow or dangerous currents, a gentle gradient and generally no big rollers.

THE EAST COAST

South of Victoria, two roads lead towards the airport. The old coast road twists and turns to follow the original coast (before reclamation work), while the East Coast Highway crosses reclaimed land, past the industrial area of **Providence** and the modern housing estate of **Roche Caiman**. On the left, a causeway leads to **Eden Island**. This reclaimed island has been set aside for the development of private residences ranging from villas to duplex apartments.

South of the airport, the road passes through **Anse aux Pins**, one of the largest villages of the Seychelles. Along the straight road from the village, look out for the attractive building of the **Kreole Institute** that is close to a turning inland, **Montagne Posée Road**. About 300m (450yds) after this turning is the **Craft Village**, an excellent place to browse for souvenirs. Opening times of individual outlets vary, with some open every day, but many closed on Sundays and public holidays. The first shop near the entrance on the right is **Maison Coco**, which as the name suggests specialises in anything and everything made out of coconut products, from bags to ornaments to boxes and beads. Carry on to the main village area, which has ample parking. At the far end is a beautiful colonial house dating from 1870, now restored as a museum. Each side of the road is lined with kiosks selling arts and crafts. There is a Creole Restaurant, Vye Marmit (open daily noon–9pm), serving local specialities such as fruit bat, fish and seafood.

Back on the main coast road, the route continues south, rising over the promontory of **Fairyland** before descending to **Anse Royale**. There is an excellent spot for swimming and snorkelling where the road reaches the beach. A current runs parallel to the coast between the mainland and tiny **Ile Souris**. This makes drift snorkelling fun, but parents should keep an eye on small children.

At the opposite end of Anse Royale village, **Les Canelles Road** crosses the island to the west coast. Take this, and after 850m (950yds) turn left onto Sweet Escott Road, then look out for a sign pointing uphill to **Jardin du Roi** ❹ (open daily 10am–5.30pm; charge). The original site, dating from the 18th century, was established as a garden for growing spice plants smuggled out of the East Indies (see box). It was later deliberately destroyed by the French during the Napoleonic wars to prevent it falling into the hands of the British. This re-creation gives us some idea of what it was like. This is a lovely peaceful corner. All the well-known and some lesser-known spices are grown together with other tropical plants. A map of the trail around the garden and

Tropical plants at Jardin du Roi

list of plants can be obtained at the reception desk. There is a small museum with a miscellany of historical artefacts, a shop and an excellent restaurant.

THE WEST COAST

Returning to the coast road, the route continues south, bending westward to cross the island at **Anse Marie-Louise**. After about a kilometre, at **Quatre Bornes** village, take the road to the left, then after a further kilometre bear right past Banyan Tree hotel to **Intendance ⑤** beach. This is a wild and beautiful beach. Swimming or body surfing can be exciting in the

SPICE ISLANDS

Pepper once commanded a higher price per ounce than gold; and the French were desperate to grow spices in their own colonies. In the 18th century the Dutch had a monopoly on this lucrative trade, due to their occupation of the Moluccas where many spices grew naturally. Anyone trying to smuggle plants or seeds was executed. Pierre Poivre (aptly named) risked his life to bring spice plants to the French settlement on Mauritius and some were transferred to Mahé, thought to be an even safer location for their cultivation. In 1772 clove, nutmeg, pepper and cinnamon were planted in the Royal Gardens at Anse Royale and lovingly tended.

Perhaps it is the descendants of those plants that now grow in the mountains of Seychelles. In the case of cinnamon, this once precious, pampered plant now grows rampant on the slopes of all the granitic islands. It is most easily recognised when in flush; the topmost leaves turn bright scarlet or bronze. Making very sure you know what it is you are nibbling, pick a leaf and take a little bite of the flesh just by the stalk. There is no mistaking that flavour. Oil is distilled from the leaves, cinnamon spice from the powdered bark.

big waves, but can also be dangerous especially from May to September. It can be just as exhilarating to simply watch the rollers sweep in with a tremendous, incessant roar, breaking on the sand with a strong burst of spray.

It is possible to explore a little further south from Anse Intendance to the pretty little bays of **Anse Cachée**, **Anse Corail** and **Anse Bazarca**, but after these the route terminates abruptly, a chain across the road preventing drivers from proceeding to **Pointe Police**, the southern

Intendance Bay from the Banyan Tree

tip of Mahé, and to **Police Bay** where there is a military station. Returning to Quatre Bornes and turning left, the road descends to the west coast at **Anse Takamaka ❻**. This is another beautiful beach, but currents can be dangerous. **Chez Batista**, right on the beach is a charming rustic thatched restaurant, a fine stop to enjoy a cold drink or a local curry or fish and pawpaw salad.

The road swings northward, rising to cliffs offering dramatic views of the sea pounding on the granite boulders below, rounding **Pointe Maravi** and descending once more to **Baie Lazare**. An anchor on a stone pedestal commemorates the 250th anniversary of the arrival of Lazare Picault. Unfortunately, it is in the wrong place. The bay was named after Lazare Picault in error: documents show that the landing was actually made 5km (3 miles) further up the coast at

Anse Boileau. Almost opposite the monument is **Varieties Boutique** which, during opening hours on sunny days, displays colourful pareos (sarongs) strung on lines between the palm trees.

At the northern end of Baie Lazare is **Gerard Devoud's Art Gallery** (www.gerarddevoud.com). Gerard Devoud uses mainly watercolours, with light and colour broken into pieces to create mosaics of landscapes and everyday village scenes. Birdwatchers might like to call in to visit the wetland adjacent to the hotel where the rare yellow bittern can be seen – the Seychelles is the only place it is found outside of Asia. Today, as the coastal marshland favoured by the birds disappears, there are perhaps fewer than 100 pairs left.

Perched on the hill above the village is Baie Lazare Church, one of the most attractive in the Seychelles. A short distance further along on the right is **Donald Adelaide's Art Studio** (open Mon–Sat from 9am to 6pm), which sells bright watercolour prints and originals beautifully depicting the islands and the Seychellois way of life.

It makes an interesting detour to get off the beaten track along **Chemin Dame Le Roi** on the right. The narrow road twists and turns into the heart of a different kind of Mahé, where former self-sufficient ways survive on smallholdings. Clothes are washed in stream water and laid out to dry on the boulders, in the traditional style. This is a reminder of how recent the modern world has arrived elsewhere in the Seychelles.

A little further along the main road, another detour is signposted on the left to Anse Soleil and a variety of

Bird life

The Indian Ocean is the only ocean closed on its northern boundary. Many of the migratory birds between Eurasia and Africa end up in Seychelles, and rarities turn up each year, especially Oct–Dec.

View over Anse la Mouche, Anse Soleil, Mt. Toupie and Baie Lazar

other attractions. The road leads to a promontory on which there are three bays: **Anse Soleil**, **Anse Gouvernement** and **Petite Anse** ❼. Anse Soleil is a delightful small sandy beach, superb for swimming with excellent views of the west coast. From the coast, follow the road for about 1km (1/2 mile) until you reach a turning to the right, signposted downhill to Anse Soleil. The road peters out close to the beach, but continues as a track to a small parking area next to **Anse Soleil Beachcomber**, where you will see a sign for the **Anse Soleil Café**. Set off on foot in the direction indicated for about 100m (110yds), turn left and follow the track between the houses to the restaurant and beach. Petite Anse, another attractive little beach, is next to Anse Soleil, but the only land access is through private grounds.

To reach Anse Gouvernement, backtrack to the junction and turn right for about 1km (1/2 mile). En route, it is worth a stop to admire the sculptures on display at Studio Antonio on the right. The beach itself is a wild and windswept bay during the southeast monsoon, not good for swimming. However, the scenery is enchanting; a beautiful sandy bay decorated with massive granite boulders.

Continuing northward on the main coast road, it passes the art studio of the Seychelles most famous artist, **Michael Adams**. His paintings are a jungle of criss-crossing leaves, stalks and stems of every hue, in a characteristic style sometimes copied but never bettered. Some pictures take an almost satirical look at Seychellois life. Excellent prints of his work are on sale at the studio, but originals are very expensive. Almost next door is the **Pineapple Studio** (open Mon–Fri 8am–4.30pm), selling a range of attractive and innovative souvenirs, including beautiful pareos, woven hessian bags and vibrantly painted coconuts. The owners live next door to the shop and will usually open up any time within reason.

Michael Adams at work in his studio

After the small cove of Anse aux Poules Bleus, the view opens up on to the wide sweeping vista of **Anse à la Mouche**. The shallow, calm waters are ideal for swimming, though you need to wade out a long way at low tide. The coast road connects with the east coast via **Les Canelles Road**. A short detour uphill along Les Canelles Road takes you to sculptor **Tom Bowers' studio** (open Mon–Sat 10am–4.30pm), signposted on the right. He uses resin for his sculptures of Seychellois, which are then cast in bronze in limited editions.

Anse à la Mouche

Back on the west coast, the road passes on through the old coconut plantation of **Barbarons**. At the north end of the beach (just after the Barbarons Hotel) there is a car park on the right for **Sentier Vacoa Trail**. The trail leads uphill alongside a stream. It is well marked and is a pleasant and fairly easy introduction to the forest, compared to the steeper mountain walks.

The former BBC World Service Relay Station with its unmistakeable masts is a short distance further on, and almost opposite there is a turning to the right, the **La Misere Road**, which leads back to the east coast. There is little of note along this road, though there are excellent viewing points overlooking both the east and west coast.

Continuing on the west coast, the road turns back towards **Grand Anse**, designated a Site of Outstanding Natural Beauty.

Granite coastline near Grand Anse

There is room to park by the school at the north end of the bay. This is good for a walk to explore the splendid, sandy beach and an attractive lagoon area at the far end where the river flows into the sea. The sea is dangerous here and is not safe for swimming. The huge rolling waves pounding the beach create a strong undertow, particularly between May and October.

From Grand Anse the road climbs uphill, emerging at the coast once more beside Mahé Beach Hotel and tiny picturesque **Petite Ile**. Three islands now come into view, rocky **Ile aux Vaches Marines**, Thérèse Island and, beyond it, the most westerly point of the granitics, **Conception Island**.

The coast road continues, passing the turning for the **Sans Souci** road to **Port Glaud**, and over a causeway through mangrove swamp, climbing to afford views over the **Port Launay Marine National Park**. The trip is a there-and-back-again drive, getting you nowhere, but certainly offers some fabulous views. It comes to an end at the gates of the Marine Park Authority headquarters at **Baie Ternay**. Turning around, the quickest way back to the east coast is via La Misere, rather than the Sans Souci road, though the latter route through the heart of **Morne Seychellois National Park** is more spectacular.

MORNE SEYCHELLOIS NATIONAL PARK

The largest National Park in the Seychelles was created in 1979. It is about 10km (6 miles) long and 2-4km (1-2 miles) wide, representing about 20 percent of the area of Mahé, stretching from sea level to the summit of **Morne Seychellois** ❽ at 905m (2,970ft). Much of the forest is secondary in nature, due to heavy exploitation in the past, with introduced trees such as cinnamon and albizia dominating. However, native plants also abound the higher you climb, and the majority of the 80 or so endemic species of the Seychelles can be found here.

GEOLOGY OF THE GRANITE ISLANDS

The granite islands of the Seychelles are unique. They are the world's only oceanic granite islands, and they are also the world's oldest ocean islands. These rocks formed three-quarters of a billion years ago and have never been submerged. A quarter of a billion years ago, they formed a part of the ancient supercontinent of Pangaea, which encompassed all the world's continents. Then around 200 million years ago, Pangaea broke up, Laurasia to the north and Gondwanaland (including the Seychelles) to the south. Around 127 million years ago Madagascar, India and the granitic Seychelles broke away from Africa, and drifted across what is now the Indian Ocean, with Madagascar breaking away about 82 million years ago. Finally, in the midst of an era famed as marking the extinction of the dinosaurs 65 million years ago, the Seychelles broke off from the western edge of India. For millennia it was a single landmass, covering 300,000 sq km (117,000 sq miles), an area larger than Britain and Ireland combined. It was still a huge single landmass as recently as 10,000 years ago during the last Ice Age when sea levels were lower than at present. Today, we can just see the tips of the mountains of this mysterious island, all that remains of it above the surface.

The cool green mountains of Mahé are a refreshing contrast to the beach. There are some excellent well-marked walks here (see page 87), but the easiest way to get a taste of the atmosphere is by hire-car or taxi, travelling across the island from one side to the other on the Sans Souci road. Even for those who are not particularly interested in natural history, it is worth traversing the mountain pass just to experience the unique feeling of a place where the silence is only intermittently disturbed by the piping of frogs, the whistling of birds and the rushing of the wind in the trees. It is here that one can appreciate the island of Mahé's remoteness as well as its ancient origins.

Starting from either **Beau Vallon** or **Victoria**, the National Park is reached by taking the **Bel Air Road** off Revolution Avenue (this route can be followed in reverse from the west coast). From here it would take about 45 minutes non-stop

Hiking in the heart of the Morne Seychellois National Park

to cross the island by car, but there are plenty of reasons to stop on the way.

The first, just 100m (110yds) on the left along the Bel Air Road, is the oldest cemetery of the Seychelles. Sadly, apart from a small plaque at the entrance, there are no informative signs. Gravestones lie strewn at random, their epitaphs often illegible, but here

Pitcher Plants

The *Nepenthes* genus of pitcher plants is a mainly Oriental family. Of 70 species in total, all but two are in southeast Asia. The exceptions are in Seychelles and Madagascar, an echo of the ancient land link that bound together these now far-flung landmasses.

lie some of the pioneers of the settlement of the island and it is an atmospheric spot. Amongst them is the tomb of Jean-Francois Hodoul, one of the more famous French corsairs who preyed on English shipping in the Napoleonic wars. In 1800 he settled on Silhouette Island and became a respected citizen of the Seychelles. The inscription on his tomb reads: 'Il fut juste' ('he was just'), and his wife Olivette is buried beside him.

Continuing uphill, the road passes **Thoughts Stained Glass Studio** on the left, where beautiful souvenirs can be purchased. Shortly after this, also on the left, is **Liberation Road**, well worth a detour to enjoy the panoramic view of Victoria, the port and the islands of St Anne Marine National Park.

Back on the Sans Souci road, the route twists and turns upward, and endemic palms, trees and screwpines start to become more frequent. The road passes signboards indicating the start of walks to **Trois Frères** and **Copolia** (see page 88), reaching almost 500m (1,640ft), before dipping towards the west coast. Look out for the first turning on the left, where it is possible to turn off the road along a rough track, parking on the right at the first bend after 50m (55yds).

A short stroll further along the track and the vista opens up over the tea plantation. On working days, women will be seen walking between the rows of tea bushes, collecting the fresh green leaves.

You may occasionally see areas of forest that have been cleared by the Forestry Division, which is attempting to control invasive tree species such as albizia and replant the slopes with native trees, several of which occur nowhere else on earth. One of the most famous in botanical circles, which survives in limited numbers and may only be seen with the aid of a guide, is the so-called jellyfish tree, which grows up on high glacis. This tree is so unusual they had to invent a genus in which to put it, and, whilst not impressive to look at, it is one of the most primitive flowering plants on earth, reminding us of the island's long isolation from the rest of the world.

Back on the main road, the next turning on the right leads uphill to **Mission Historical Ruins and Viewing Point**. Turn right here and park at the top. Little is left here, save for the vestiges of a few buildings, from what was originally called **Venn's Town**, where missionaries ran a board-ing school for the children of the liberated Africans landed in Seychelles after 1861 (see page 18). They were given a basic education and taught a trade prior to being apprenticed or sent into service. It was perhaps not as dour an institution as it sounds. Marianne North, an intrepid Victorian visitor who saw Venn's Town after

View of the west coast from Mission

an ascent of the mountain track on a donkey, as was necessary in those days before roads, said that 'the silence of the forest around was only broken by the children's happy voices'.

From the steps that lead up from the car park, follow the path between the trees. This used to be a magnificent avenue of huge sangdragon trees, but they fell victim to a disease in 2003. In time, the young endemic trees planted by the Ministry of Environment will take their place. Situated at the end of the short path is a

Worker at the tea factory

sheltered viewing platform, which affords the most dazzling view in the Seychelles, over the green hillsides to the west coast and the deep waters of the Indian Ocean. This viewing point was erected for the visit of Queen Elizabeth II in 1972. Often, even when it is clear and sunny at sea level, misty clouds settle on the mountain tops, or roll down the valleys bringing a damp atmospheric chill. Nowadays the silence is pierced by the high-pitched peep of unseen frogs in the leaf litter and the nasal squawks of bulbuls, rather than the voices of children.

Back on the main road and continuing to the west coast, the surrounding slopes are planted with tea, and the **Seychelles Tea & Coffee Company** is soon reached, a pleasant stop for refreshments. The locally grown tea is excellent. On weekday mornings it is also possible to take a tour of the tea factory.

ISLANDS TO VISIT FROM MAHÉ

Anonyme ❾, just offshore near the International Airport, has a small resort but can also be visited for the day or for a half-day when the whole island is not hired. Call Anonyme Island Resort (tel: 4380100/710111) and arrange a time to be collected by boat from their jetty, just north of the airport on the reclaimed land.

On the island there is a swimming pool, nice beaches for swimming (though the water is shallow at low tide), a nature trail around the island, snorkelling equipment and kayaks. It is usually possible to kayak across to the nearby deserted **Rat Island** (where there are actually no rats because they were all eradicated in 2005) in about 30 minutes, but ask the staff about sea conditions before doing so. Lunch or dinner at the *Piment Vert* restaurant can be arranged with flexible meal times.

St Anne Island now has the private grounds of a five-star resort in one corner, but most of the island retains a wild character. The first settlers lived on this island, clearing a patch of marshland in which to plant their crops. It seems there

St Anne Island and it's Beachcomber Hotel

are no physical traces of this settlement remaining, but it is still easy to imagine how it might have appeared.

The small islands of **Round** and **Moyenne** in the St Anne Marine National Park, and the larger island of **Cerf**, can easily be visited by small boat or glass-bottom boat from Victoria.

Tiny Round Island (2 hectares/5 acres) can be circumnavigated in less than 10 minutes' walk. Moyenne is somewhat larger (9 hectares/22 acres), with a nature trail that takes about 45 minutes to walk. Cerf Island is much bigger (127 hectares/314 acres), covered in coconut palms and scrub, and has several trails that run up the hill if you want to explore

inland. All three islands are excellent for swimming and all have small restaurants.

PRASLIN

Praslin, 45km (28 miles) northeast of Mahé, is the Seychelles' second-largest granitic island in both size and population. It has a gentler profile, reaching just 367m (1,204ft). The hills appear rather threadbare compared to Mahé's mountains, but the primeval palm forests of the valleys are found nowhere else on earth. All six endemic palms are found here, including the island's symbol, coco de mer. The roads are quieter than on Mahé and the pace of life is slower.

No trip to Praslin is complete without a visit to the World Heritage Site of **Vallée de Mai** ⑩ (open daily 8am–5.30pm; ticket sales end 5pm; charge), the world's largest forest of coco de mer. Even if you have no interest in flora and fauna,

Vallée de Mai Nature Reserve

the atmosphere of the place is inspiring. The valley occupies the heart of Praslin, halfway between **Grande Anse** and **Baie St Anne**. At the entrance there is a shop where tickets and souvenirs may be purchased. An excellent guide leaflet is included with the admission fee, which helps support the work of Seychelles Islands

Coco de mer

Female coco de mer trees bear the world's largest nut, with an uncanny resemblance to the female pelvis. The enormous catkin of the male tree is also suggestive. Some public toilets use nut and catkin symbols to indicate which is the gents and which is the ladies.

Foundation, managers of the valley and of the Seychelles' other World Heritage Site, Aldabra.

Several nature trails run through the valley. These are well marked and maintained and are shown clearly in the free leaflet. Options include a short tour taking in most of the botanical sites (lasting about an hour), or a longer circular route (two to three hours at a leisurely pace) which includes a spectacular viewpoint where black parrots and Seychelles cave swiftlets may often be seen. Walking is easy, and though the path rises and falls, it is not too steep.

About a quarter of the trees in the valley are coco de mer palms, and almost half the remainder are other palms found only in the Seychelles. All six endemic palms of the Seychelles are found in Vallée de Mai along with the national bird, the Seychelles black parrot, which also breeds only on Praslin. The silence of the valley is broken by the piercing whistle of the black parrot, but the birds are often difficult to locate in the dense forest. They are most easily seen in more open areas, including close to the entrance and from the viewing point.

The British general, Charles Gordon, visiting the valley in 1881, concluded that this valley was the Garden of Eden, and the coco de mer the Tree of Knowledge. While some might dismiss his religious theories, few could dispute that the coco de mer nut resembles the thighs and belly of a woman. There are male and female trees, the male trees having huge and extraordinarily phallic catkins.

THE COAST

The coast road north from the airport at Amitié leads past **Anse Kerlan** to the gates of Constance Lemuria Resort. Anse Kerlan can sometimes be rough, and currents are strong during the northwest monsoon, but on calmer days it is excellent for swimming and snorkelling. Lemuria Resort has the only 18-hole golf course in the Seychelles and very attractive grounds. **Anse Georgette**, also within the grounds, is one of the most beautiful beaches of the Seychelles.

At Amitié, opposite the airstrip by the sea, is the **Black Pearl Praslin Ocean Farm** (open Mon–Fri 10am–4pm, Sat 10am–noon; tel: 233150; charge). The main business of the farm is the culture of black pearls in oyster beds between

MAGIC TREES

The local superstition is that on stormy moonlit nights the coco de mer trees come alive and make love like men and women. The tree is surrounded by myths; even its name is based in legend. It was believed the tree grew beneath the sea, because although nuts occasionally turned up on foreign shores, no one had ever found the tree from which they came, until the French visited Praslin. The mystery behind the nut's origins led people to attribute it with marvellous powers. Kings and potentates, including Russian tsars, had the shell made into fabulous cups, set in gold, to drink from; they believed that the nut could neutralise poison.

The perfect spot to moor up

Praslin and Curieuse, and the sale of jewellery incorporating the pearls in beautiful gold and silver settings. These are extremely attractive, but expensive. There is also an aquarium touch pool, with concrete tanks displaying corals, reef fish and invertebrates.

Grand Anse is the largest settlement on Praslin, but it is a quiet place compared to the larger villages of Mahé. There are several hotels, restaurants and takeaways here, though heavy seaweed on the beach makes it a little less picturesque than elsewhere. Black parrots can sometimes be seen in the tall mango and breadfruit trees behind the Britannia Hotel, 200m (220yds) inland from the parish **Church of St Matthew**.

From Grand Anse the coast road continues southward past the junction at **Fond de L'Anse** and the turning to Vallée de Mai, past a series of eight beautiful bays. This is a wonderfully tranquil stretch of coast, though not the best for swimming due to the shallow waters, except close to high tide. The first bay is **Anse Citron**, followed by **Anse Bateau**, with the thatched building of Les Rochers Restaurant. A further 750m (825yds) after the restaurant is Villa Flamboyant at **Anse St Sauveur**. This small, charismatic guesthouse is a great place to see black parrots, especially in the early morning or late afternoon. There is also a gallery selling prints of paintings by former owner Verney Cresswell. Beyond Villa Flamboyant is **Anse Takamaka**, followed by **Anse Cimitière** and **Anse Bois de Rose**, where Black Parrot Restaurant and Coco de Mer Hotel are the only substantial establishments on this entire stretch of coast.

Rounding **Pointe Cocos**, the southern tip of Praslin, the road reaches **Anse Consolation** followed by **Anse Marie Louise**,

PIROGUES

The origins of the traditional Seychelles fishing boat, the pirogue, are uncertain. Perhaps the original was modelled on African river canoes modified for local use in shallow seas, ideal for skimming over reefs and landing on surf beaches due to their shallow draught. They were normally powered by oars, but on good days the men raised a '*voile coco*' described as 'a coconut leaf plaited in the form of a sail'. Pirogues were built from takamaka wood, the ends shaped from sections of solid tree trunk, the centre from two separate pieces, fitted together with copper tacks, seams caulked, to form crafts of between 4–11m (15–36ft) depending upon their purpose, then painted in the traditional black and white livery. One writer described them as 'leaking patchwork quilts always in need of caulking cotton, copper sheet, *blanc d'espagne*, linseed oil, blacking, copper tacks and wood...'

Before the arrival of the marine engine, it could take 30 hours to row to La Digue from Mahé. The men sang as they rowed, and at dusk those waiting ashore to buy fish would hear the singing drifting out of the darkness towards them as the pirogues approached.

which is good for swimming, except at low tide. An unmarked track inland leads to **Fond Ferdinand**, similar in character to Vallée de Mai but much wilder without the well-marked pathways. The road then turns steeply uphill, passing the up-market Chateau de Feuilles Hotel and Restaurant before the view of **Baie St Anne** opens up and the road descends to the village. The jetty here is the terminal for inter-island ferries to Mahé and La Digue schooners. Many charter boats and local fishing boats moor within the wide arms of

Black parrot

the bay. Praslin attracts art lovers and artists. A little further on, at the edge of the village, a sign points to **Cap Samy Art Gallery** (open Tues–Sat 10am–4pm; tel: 4 232048), 300m (330yds) up a steep hill.

At the north end of the bay the main road swings inland and the road straight ahead leads to **Anse La Blague ⑪**. After 1.2km (3/4 mile) you pass the Isles des Palmes beach bungalows and the **Art Gallery and Giant Tortoise Park** (open daily 9am–5pm). The gallery exhibits the interesting Seychelles panoramas and nature originals of local artist Raymond Dubuisson, but the tortoise park is just a rather grand name for a slightly larger than average tortoise pen. After a further 1km (1/2 mile), the road dips to the beach, where the fine Vanille Restaurant sits on a terrace overlooking the sea

Fish Stand, Côte D'Or

and there is a snack bar on the beach. Diving, windsurfing and jet surfing can be arranged by Bleu Marine, based at the small hotel here. Just beyond the hotel 25m (30yds) uphill is the home and art gallery of **'Robinson' Sey Marx** (open daily 7am–6pm), offering reasonably priced original paintings.

Returning to the junction at Baie St Anne, the straight inland road passes through woodland, comprising of mainly takamaka, Indian almond and casuarina species, to Tante Mimi Restaurant on the right. Next to the restaurant, within the same grounds is **George Camille Art Gallery** (open Mon–Fri 10am–6pm, Sat 9am–1pm).

Beyond Tante Mimi is **Côte d'Or**, Praslin's equivalent of Beau Vallon with many hotels and marine-based activities. Sheltered by **Curieuse Island**, the 3km (2 miles) long beach is excellent for swimming year-round, including for children. The beach shelves very gradually so it is necessary to walk out a long way at low tide to find water deep enough for swimming. The best snorkelling is around the boulders at the northern end of the beach and out towards **Chauve Souris Island**. There are several boats available for hire offering trips to nearby islands or just around the corner and the beaches of Anse Lazio and Anse Georgette.

The inland turning just before MCB Bank soon returns to the coast at the north end of the bay at Paradise Sun Hotel. Passing **Pointe Zanguilles** at the north end of Côte d'Or, you reach Anse Possession, a beautiful bay that takes its name from the fact that in 1768 the first French explorers erected a plaque here, claiming possession of the island. Continuing northward, the road passes through takamaka and casuarina woodland to **Anse Boudin**, then rises over the headland to descend to **Anse Lazio**, which vies with Anse Source d'Argent (on La Digue) in many polls to be 'the best beach in the world'. Its reputation has gone before it and it has become relatively crowded, with quite a few charter boats usually anchored here, except in strong northwest winds. Nevertheless, it is still a beautiful spot and the swimming and snorkelling are excellent. Snorkelling is best around the rocks at the corners of the bay. There are two restaurants: Bonbon Plume, with thatched umbrellas dotted across a lawn by the sea, and, at the opposite end of the beach, Le Chevalier Restaurant, set back from the shoreline. Both offer mainly seafood and Creole cuisine.

Anse Lazio

LA DIGUE

La Digue is just under half the size of Praslin in terms of both area and population. It used to be known as the land that time forgot, but one measure of how far this has changed is the presence of three internet cafés within a short distance of the jetty. The main form of public transport was the ox cart, but motorised vehicles are now common. Ox carts survive, but perhaps their days are numbered. Nevertheless, an island total of just a few taxis is hardly crowded and La Digue retains a delightfully gentle character. Most people – tourists and locals alike – get around by bike and no one ever seems to be in a hurry. Many of the locals are descended from revolutionaries deported from the French island of Reunion in the 1790s. They were destined for India, but took matters into their own hands and rerouted for the island instead.

LA PASSE TO L'UNION ESTATE

Most of the residents and tourist facilities are centred on the west coast close to La Passe, the arrival point for the vast majority, though a few come by helicopter. There are regular ferries to Praslin, just 30 minutes away, so it is possible to visit without staying overnight. If taking this option, book a ferry in advance as they are sometimes full, especially on weekends and public holidays.

La Passe jetty is an artificial harbour creating shelter for visiting yachts and schooners. Ashore, there is

Plantation Houses

The island's plantation houses were built on stone piers allowing the breeze to pass underneath the main living space. Walls finished short of the ceiling to let air circulate from room to room, and the veranda wrapped around the building so there was always a cool spot to recline in.

Anse Source D'Argent Beach

a tourist information office and a small cafeteria, Tarosa Café (open daily 10.30am-2pm and 6.30-8pm). On the opposite side of the road there are plenty of bicycles available for hire and this is the best way to see La Digue. Standards are generally good, but it is wise to examine a few first before deciding on a particular model.

If bikes are not your thing, the flat coastal plateau and its beaches as far as **L'Union Estate** to the south of La Passe is easily explored on foot. Along the way, there are several grand old plantation houses. La Digue experienced a golden age when vanilla was the number-one export and there were several very successful plantations here. Some growers made small fortunes and built themselves these beautiful homes.

The road turns inland to bypass La Digue Island Lodge then runs parallel to the coast to a T-junction at Pont Bill. Turn left down Pont Bill for about 100m (110yds) to the **Veuve Reserve** (open daily, free). Veuve, or 'widow', is the local name

Belle Vue

of the beautiful Seychelles paradise flycatcher, the long black tail feathers of the male reminiscent of a widow's black veil. The female by contrast is chestnut and white with a black hood, lacking the extravagant tail feathers. The bird breeds only on La Digue and is the symbol of the island, and the reserve protects the once widespread takamaka and Indian almond woodland, where it still thrives. It may be seen most easily in the early morning or late afternoon. There is a small **visitors centre** with displays about the bird and other wildlife, and the warden can provide help if needed on where to find the flycatchers.

Inland from the reserve, the road bends back on itself to run northward. A further 100m (110yds) from the turning is **Chateau St Cloud**, a delightful old building, once part of a vanilla farm, now a small hotel. Near to the Chateau, a steep road leads to **Belle Vue**. This is impossible to cycle and not easy to walk, especially in the middle of the day. However, the energetic are rewarded with a magnificent view over the coastal plateau and across the sea to Praslin. If it is too much to walk, it is well worth a taxi fare. Back at the Chateau and continuing north, the road turns downhill and regains the coast, emerging close to La Passe jetty once more.

West of the Veuve Reserve, the road leads back to the coast and turns southward. It passes **Green Gecko Art & Craft Shop** (open Mon–Sat 10am–12.30pm, 1.30–6pm) selling a variety of works, followed by the picturesque **Roman Catholic church** then **Barbara Jenson's Studio** (open Mon–Sat 10am–6pm), where attractive original work in aluminium and acrylics is displayed. Shortly after the studio, the road forks: take the coastal route straight on to **L'Union Estate** (open daily 8am– 5pm; charge). The estate is an open-air museum of plantation life, including a working *kalorifer*, used to make copra (dried coconut), an ox-powered coconut oil press and vanilla pro- cessing. Other features include the La Digue Rock, a gigantic boulder like a natural sculpture, giant tortoises, horse riding

THE COCONUT INDUSTRY

Copra is the flesh of the coconut from which coconut oil is ex- tracted. The nuts are harvested and de-husked, the shells cracked open and the flesh removed in chunks, which are laid on racks in the kalorifer or copra drier. The empty shells fuel a furnace from which a metal pipe runs the length of the drier. The copra is dried over several days in the hot dry air. In earlier times an ox-powered oil mill was used for oil extraction. This mill was a giant mor- tar and pestle; the 'pestle' connected by a yoke to the ox which walked round in a circle, thus pressing the copra against the side of the mortar and squeezing the oil out. Cup copra was exported in the past; the coconut was cut in half and the flesh left inside forming a cup which was widely used in Hindu ceremonies. The Seychelles' copra is of particularly fine quality, and the nuts here never have to be harvested by climbing the tree as they have to in some parts of the world. In the Seychelles they obligingly fall to the ground at the perfect moment.

Trekking from Grand Anse to Petit Anse

and a picturesque plantation house (now a private home). The estate also guards the entrance to La Digue's most famous beach, **Anse Source D'Argent** ⑫, meaning Silver Spring Bay. The beach has frequently been named as the best in the world. It is worth going as early in the morning to see it at its best.

GRAND ANSE

Near the entrance to L'Union Estate, the road turns inland through a flat marshy area, **La Mare Soupap** (*Soupap* is the Creole name for the terrapins to be found here). It then climbs steeply before descending to **Grand Anse** ⑬. The views en route are stunning, as is the beach itself, though it can be dangerous to swim here especially during the strong winds of June to September. There is a bar and restaurant, Loutier Coco (bar open daily 9am–5pm, restaurant 12.30–3pm) serving a Creole buffet at lunchtimes. A track leads northeast towards two more beautiful bays, **Petite Anse** and **Anse Cocos**. The track is not navigable by bike but is easy on foot.

Unless you are particularly adventurous it is not worth exploring further than Anse Cocos. The track turns inland, crossing **Pointe Ma Flore** to **Anse Caiman**. There it peters out, and it can be a struggle to reach the road at **Anse Fourmis**, even though it is little more than a further 200m (220yds). This is easier at low tide on calm days when you may wade through the shallow water; it is not much fun at other times when a precarious scramble over slippery granite boulders pounded by waves may be required.

LA PASSE TO ANSE FOURMIS

North of La Passe, the road rounds the top of the island and leads to Anse Fourmis, a distance of about 4km (2 miles). There are several beautiful beaches en route, the first of which, **Anse Severe**, is one of the best on La Digue for swimming and snorkelling, except when there is a strong onshore wind. Snorkelling is easiest within a couple of hours either side of high tide and the best place is around the rocks at the corner of the beach. Beyond the northern tip of La Digue is **Anse Patates**. This is a rocky bay but it is also good for swimming and snorkelling. Next is **Anse Gaulettes**, where swimming can be dangerous because of strong currents,

Snorkelling at Anse Source d'Argent

then **Anse Grosse Roche**, named after the immense granite outcrop at the northern end of the bay, and **Anse Banane**, both safe for swimming though the sea can be rough at times. At Anse Fourmis, the road ends. Snorkelling is good when the sea is calm around the rocks.

ISLANDS NEAR PRASLIN AND LA DIGUE

Praslin is a great base for day or half-day trips to several other islands. Tours to all of these islands can be booked through almost any Praslin hotel, with tour operators, or direct with boat owners. It is also possible to visit these islands from La Digue, but Praslin offers more options and shorter transit times to most. Some boat operators require a minimum of anything up to eight persons for some island visits. Among the best options are Louis Bedier (tel: 4232157), Basil Ferrari (tel: 4233411), Edwin Rose (tel: 252298) and Dream Yacht (tel: 4232681).

ARIDE

To see the nearest thing to what the Seychelles looked like before humans arrived, head for **Aride Island Nature Reserve** ⑭ (tel: 4321600; open Sun-Thu, Fri and Sat by appointment

View from Anse Lazio, Pointe Chevalier to Aride Island

only; charge). This is the most northerly of the granitic islands. Its size and relative isolation mean that a full-day trip is required, but this also means fewer people compared to other island trips, and more time to savour the beauty of the place, take photographs, swim, snorkel (450 fish species have been recorded), explore or relax. Sometimes it is difficult to land, especially during May to September. If in doubt, call the warden to check local conditions.

Fairy tern on Aride Island

Aride is the largest island never to be invaded by rats, which elsewhere arrived with humans and devastated the wildlife on ocean islands throughout the world. Rats can climb and will kill chicks and eat the eggs of tree-nesting species. Because several seabird species nest on the ground, they are particularly vulnerable to attack by rats, and they have decimated seabird populations where they are present. As a result of their absence, Aride has more seabirds of more species than the other 40 granite islands of the Seychelles added together. Five of the 12 endemic land birds of the Seychelles breed here. Unlike most islands, it is not dominated by coconuts, and plants include the beautiful fragrant shrub Wright's gardenia, found naturally nowhere else on earth. Historical interest includes one of the few remaining plantation houses and a pirogue (once the main form of inter-island transport).

The island is owned by the Royal Society of Wildlife Trusts of UK and leased and managed by local NGO, the Island

Conservation Society. The Aride Island Conservation Centre features exhibits on the history and natural history of the island. A limited selection of sales items helps fund some of the longest continuous scientific monitoring programmes undertaken in the Seychelles.

A nature trail leads through a small plantation area where the warden and staff grow a few crops to supplement their diet. The rest of the island is given over to nature. The walk along the plateau is easy. It then turns uphill and, while not too steep, can be hot work on humid days, but the effort is

FRIGATE BIRDS

Frigate birds look like pterodactyls, yet they are highly evolved. Unlike almost every other seabird, males are dramatically different to females, with bizarre scarlet inflatable pouches for display. They have the lowest wing-load factor (mass to wing area) of any bird and hollow flexible bones that make up just five percent of their total weight, enabling them to soar effortlessly even on calm days. Frigate birds have tiny legs and cannot even walk on land, only perch. They cannot even land on water, their weak legs and unwebbed feet providing insufficient propulsion to take off again. All their food is taken on the wing. The birds have fused pectoral girdle bones, giving them tremendous aerial agility for catching flying fish or harrying boobies.

Frigate birds travel 650km (400 miles) on fishing trips during nesting, and when not breeding they cross entire oceans. They take longer to reach maturity than any other bird species (10–12 years) and have the longest breeding cycle, a full year. Most curiously, DNA studies put them in the same super-family as penguins! So, the tropical, ultimate masters of flight that cannot swim are related to polar, flightless, swimming maestros!

worth it. The view from the northern cliffs at the climax of the trail is stunning. There is no comparable cliff-top view in the Seychelles and nowhere else is it possible to look down upon thousands of roosting frigate birds, and glimpse the elusive red-tailed tropicbird, while in the turquoise waters below, rays, turtles and dolphins may clearly be seen.

COUSIN

Cousin Island Nature Reserve is owned by BirdLife International and managed by Nature Seychelles (open

Hawksbill turtle hatchlings, Cousin

Mon–Fri 10am until noon; tel: Cousin 2718816, Mahe 4601100; charge). It is a smaller, gentler version of Aride, without the huge number of frigate birds but with the same land birds and many of the seabird species. It is also largely rehabilitated to its natural state since its purchase as a reserve in 1968. Cousin is only 2km (1 mile) from Praslin and fairly sheltered with a beach surrounding most of the island so that landing is generally possible all year round.

Visitors cannot land themselves (a measure implemented to prevent the introduction of pests). This must be done by disembarking into the island's small boats. On open days, a small armada of boats from Praslin moors offshore and waits for the island's boats to come out to collect and ferry visitors ashore, who then assemble at the boat shelter. This process can take an hour or so, depending on the number of people to be landed and your place in the queue. The gathered ensemble is then split into English- or French-speaking groups for guided tours around the island. The tour lasts about 2 hours. It is not possible to roam the island unaccompanied and there is no time to swim or snorkel, but trips are very well organised and led by knowledgeable guides. Most of the birds are very tame and can be photo-graphed at close quarters.

Cousin is one of the most important hawksbill turtle nest-ing islands in the western Indian Ocean and has a long tradi-tion of turtle monitoring. During the nesting season (Oct–Apr) there is quite a good chance of seeing one, as they will come ashore to nest in daylight, unlike in other parts of the world. Nesting turtles should never be approached until they have begun to lay, and, even then, only under the watchful eye of one of the island's staff.

CURIEUSE AND ST PIERRE

An excursion to Cousin is often combined with a visit to **Curieuse Island** for lunch and to nearby **St Pierre** islet for

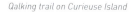
Qalking trail on Curieuse Island

snorkelling. You can also arrange separate day trips to Curieuse Island from most Praslin hotels. Curieuse lies just 1km (1/2 mile) north of Praslin at the centre of a Marine National Park. It is less heavily wooded than other islands and was once known as Ile Rouge because from the sea the red soil is very noticeable. A leper

Snorkelling excursion to St. Pierre Island

colony was established here in 1833 at **Anse St José**. Ruins of the lepers' houses remain, while the doctor's house has been renovated as a Visitors Centre with an excellent history section on the ground floor and a reasonably good natural history section on the first floor. Next to the doctor's house there are sheltered tables and an area for barbecues.

A footpath leads over the hill to **Baie Laraie**. Apart from the steep hill at the start of the walk, this is a very easy stroll. It used to be possible to walk across the causeway that had previously enclosed live turtles prior to export, but this was largely destroyed in the 2004 tsunami and the remains can still be seen. The path follows the coast, part of it a boardwalk through mangroves of various species. At Baie Laraie there is a Tortoise Conservation Project, where baby tortoises are kept in pens to give them a head start in life before being released. The turtle pond has also become a sanctuary for female lemon sharks to birth their offspring and is another conservation project.

Aerial view of Grand Soeur Island

THE SISTERS, ILE COCOS AND MARIANNE

Grand Soeur and neighbouring **Petit Soeur** (known collectively as The Sisters; charge) are owned by the Praslin hotel Château de Feuilles, which reserves them exclusively for guests at weekends. During the week, other boat owners offer trips usually with a barbecue lunch and the opportunity for snorkelling. The island boat ferries guests ashore to Grand Soeur. There are sandy beaches on each side, so that landing is possible in both seasons. It lacks the rich wildlife of Aride and Cousin, but is a beautiful little island with nice beaches, and the snorkelling is excellent.

Nearby, tiny **Ile Cocos** (2 hectares/5 acres) is surrounded by a small Marine National Park (charge) and has one of the best snorkelling sites in the granitics. There are large numbers of parrotfish, butterflyfish, angelfish and groupers. Whale sharks are sometimes seen in this vicinity. **Marianne** is nearly 2km (1 mile) north of Cocos. It is covered with a monoculture of coconuts but is fun to visit because it is uninhabited. A single beach on the western coast permits landings by small boat.

SILHOUETTE ISLAND

Silhouette ⓫ lies 20km (12 miles) north of Mahé. It is the third-largest island of the granitic group and the fifth-largest in the Seychelles, yet the population is tiny and the human impact is much less significant here than elsewhere. Day trips can be arranged through The Boat House at Beau Vallon, Mahé (tel: 247898), or by air through ZilAir (tel: 4375100). It is also possible to visit by private yacht, for which permission must be obtained from the government's Islands Development Company (IDC; tel: 4384640).

Though superficially similar to the other granitic islands, the rocks of Silhouette and North islands are much younger and made up largely of a type of volcanic rock called syenite dating from 63 million years ago. In the southeast of the island, between **Point Ramasse Tout** and **Point Zeng Zeng**, lies the only surface volcanic ash in the Seychelles.

The first recorded landing in the Seychelles took place here in 1609, yet the island was not settled by Europeans until the early 19th century. The island's name honours the French Controller-General of Finances in 1759, Etienne de Silhouette, who was said to have implemented such severe fiscal policies that they reduced people to shadows of their former selves, hence the origin of the word silhouette. One of the first

Sunset over Silhouette Island

distinguished residents was the corsair Hodoul, who was recorded as having settled here in 1801.

The summit of Mount Dauban rises to 740m (2,428ft) and is the second-highest summit in the Seychelles. It is one of the most important biodiversity hotspots in the Indian Ocean. For a century, until 1960, the island belonged to the Dauban family, under whom attempts were made to develop agriculture and forestry and the population reached 1,000. Many coconuts were planted, often in seemingly inaccessible locations because land was deemed only to be of any value if 'under coconuts'. Breadfruit trees were also planted, the Dauban family insisting that every household should plant a tree as a source of nourishment. The Dauban era came to an end when Henri Dauban sold the island to a French hotel group and the government took possession of the island in 1983.

Anse La Passe, Silhouette Island

La Passe is the main set-tlement and has a small harbour overlooked by the Grande Case, a typical island plantation house. The Nature Protection Trust of Seychelles (NPTS) has its headquarters nearby. Proj-ects include captive breed-ing programmes for giant tortoises and terrapins. Beyond the tortoise pens, a track rounds a small marsh where grey heron and black-crowned night heron may be

Dauban Mausoleum

seen, and continues to the **Dauban Mausoleum**, a grand, somewhat incongruous construction; a monument to the eccentricities of the Dauban family. There is an easy walk from the left-hand corner of the mausoleum uphill. NPTS have planted a number of rare endemic plants here, a small step towards restoring the island, and a short guidebook is available from their visitors centre. The nature trail rejoins the main track, which leads uphill then descends to **Anse Lascars**. This is a lovely secluded bay. From here, the path winds uphill to a viewing point at the headland of **Point Zeng Zeng**. It then descends to the secluded bay of Anse Patates with its fascinating mature mangrove swamp and beach crest of windswept sea hibiscus. Returning towards La Passe, look out for the path on the right to **Anse Cimitière**, site of the old cemetery.

North of La Passe lies another beautiful empty beach, **Baie Cipailles**. From here, two paths lead to **Anse Mondon**. The lower path is overgrown and best avoided. The upper path is easier and more interesting, passing uphill through shaded native forest. Just before the descent back to the coast, the forest opens up to reveal a stunning view of Anse Mondon, where the snorkelling is excellent.

Grande Barbe lies on the opposite side to La Passe, with which it is connected by a track over the mountain. The marsh behind the plateau is the largest surviving wetland in Seychelles. An old path from Grande Barbe to Anse Mondon is still marked on some maps but it has now vanished and this walk is no longer possible.

PRIVATE ISLANDS

Several of the smaller islands are the exclusive domain of guests of the single tourism facility on them. It is legal for anyone to land on any beach at any time in the Seychelles, but the land above the high tide line is private. **Frégate Island** is the largest of these at 219 hectares (541.16 acres). Frégate is the most isolated of the granitic islands, 55km (34 miles) east of Mahé. For many years it was a thriving plantation, with a small hotel based around the plantation house. In 1998, a new up-market hotel opened. There are several beautiful beaches, watersports and a network of pathways to explore on foot or by golf cart.

Picnic on the beach, Frégate Island

North Island lies 7km (4 miles) north of Silhouette. Most of its forest was removed during years of exploitation, though a few endemic screwpines survive on high ledges. A restoration programme is now underway, and in 2005 it became the largest tropical island in the world to have rats eradicated. There is a beautiful beach on each side of the island, separated by a plateau across the middle and rocky promontories either end.

Félicité Island lies 3km (1½ miles) northeast of La Digue and its luxurious accommodation is reserved for just a few visitors. It is owned and managed by the operators of La

Leaving Bird Island by plane

Digue Island Lodge. The facilities of the Lodge include boat trips and game fishing. There is a good beach for swimming at La Penice near the Lodge, and snorkelling is also good in the same vicinity.

Cousine Island lies off Praslin, a short distance from Cousin. It is a privately owned nature reserve and is the only granite island of any size with no alien mammals, the island being exclusive for up to eight guests accommodated in four individual villas. For those who can afford it, it is a rare opportunity to experience living on an island teeming with wildlife. A resident conservation officer is available to take guests on guided walks and explain the various conservation projects.

CORAL ISLANDS WITH ACCOMMODATION

It would be a pity to visit the Seychelles and not experience at least one of the sparsely inhabited, remote flat coral islands, by way of a contrast to the granitics. There are flights most days (depending on demand) to Bird, Denis, Desroches and Alphonse. Each of these islands has a single hotel for accommodation, and day trips are not possible as flights are on the ground for a matter of minutes before returning to Mahé.

BIRD ISLAND

A 30-minute flight from Mahé is **Bird Island** ⓰, a wonderful place to relax in simple but comfortable surroundings at Bird Island Lodge. Visitors may wander all over the 101-hectare (250-acre) coral cay, provided they do not harm or disturb the wildlife. This includes the massive sooty tern colony of more than a million birds that may be seen from March to October and gives the island its name. As the most northerly Seychelles island, Bird is also the first landfall for rare migrants, especially during October to March. More migratory species have been recorded on Bird than on any other Seychelles island.

Under the guidance of a resident Conservation Officer, it is possible to see hawksbill turtles that come ashore to lay between October and March, and green turtles from April to October. Apart from nature-watching, visitors can enjoy snorkelling over the shallow reefs (in the safe regions designated), go game fishing, play table tennis or billiards, or just relax. Permanent inhabitants include Esmeralda, an enormous male giant land tortoise, once celebrated in the *Guinness Book of Records* as the heaviest in the world.

Young Islands

In contrast to the great antiquity of the granitics, Bird Island and Denis Island may be only 2,000–4,000 years old. They emerged due to a local fall in sea levels caused by a change in ocean currents around this time.

DENIS ISLAND

Denis Island  is 30 minutes by air from Mahé. The 143-hectare (353-acre) island is criss-crossed by many foot-paths and nature trails where Seychelles warblers and Seychelles fodies (introduced in 2004) can be seen. Once a coconut plantation, the island is being rehabilitated. Interesting sites on the island include the old lighthouse and cemetery. Activities include wind-surfing, canoeing, diving, nature walks and tennis. Game fishing charters and bottom fishing are available year-round.

ALPHONSE AND ST FRANCOIS ATOLL

Alphonse ⑱ is the most remote island with a hotel, 400km (250 miles) south by southwest of Mahé, 60 minutes by air. Alphonse Island Resort offers facilities for diving on the wall of Alphonse where forests of Gorgonian fan corals,

Nature trail on Denis Island

huge schools of pelagic fish and many colourful reef fish may be seen. Once a highly productive plantation, little remains as a reminder of these days save for a few old buildings and the island's cemetery near to **Pointe Huto**.

Cycles are available for every visitor and it is an easy ride to the farthest tips of the island, named after ships. **Point Doille** recalls

Winter's Retreat

Ian Fleming, creator of James Bond, came to Seychelles in 1958 and visited many islands including Alphonse where the wife of the former island manager remembers him sitting quietly on the veranda scribbling away for hours in a notebook. He based a short story, *Hildebrand's Rarity*, in the Seychelles.

a guano vessel which used to call here, though islanders knew this area as Pointe Dot, after a French coal steamer which sank off here in 1873. **Point Tamatav** is named after the *Tamatave* which came to grief here in 1903.

Boat trips are available to nearby Bijoutier for picnics, swimming and snorkelling. The lagoon of St Francois is famous for bonefishing, widely acknowledged as the best in the world, while fly-fishermen also target milkfish and trevally. The enormous flat plain of sand, left dry at low tide, is a feeding ground for hundreds of crab plovers and other waders. A feature of St Francois is the number of shipwrecks that litter the reef. Just 1km (1/2 mile) offshore, the waters are almost 5km (3 miles) deep, the wrecks standing as grim reminders of the perils of underestimating the sea.

DESROCHES

Desroches ❶❾ is the largest island of the Amirantes (394 hectares/974 acres). At 230km (144 miles) from Mahé, 45

Beach on Desroches Island

minutes by air, it is the closest island of the Amirantes to the granitics. It is the exposed rim of a huge lagoon, so deep that even cruiseships can enter and anchor close to the shore. Swimming is excellent, unlike most atolls where waters over the surrounding reef are very shallow. The beaches are also excellent.

The Settlement, 2km (1 mile) from the hotel, with its copra drier, oil press and lockup, is a reminder of the old plantation days.

Activities include sailing, cycling, canoeing, windsurfing, snorkelling deep-sea fishing and diving. Desroches is famous for the Desroches Drop with its fantastic caves, which may be explored under the supervision of a PADI dive-master. The diving is excellent, especially from November to April, though during the strong winds of the southeast monsoon, opportunities are more limited. Bird life includes grey francolin, introduced as gamebirds during the 19th century to many islands but now surviving only here and on Coetivy.

ROBINSON CRUSOE ISLANDS

Due to distance and the absence of scheduled flights (though a few islands have grassy airstrips), most of the far-flung islands to the south and west of Mahé can only be visited by charter boats. There are few places on earth left like these beautiful, remote, mostly uninhabited islands. Some may be developed for tourism one day. Meanwhile, those who make the journey will feel privileged to visit such pristine islands.

THE AMIRANTES

Apart from Desroches and Alphonse, the islands of the Amirantes have no accommodation and are mostly uninhabited. They can only be visited by live-aboard boats at present. **African Banks** in the north is almost treeless, but a haven for nesting terns. **Rémire** is a Presidential retreat and ordinarily impossible to visit. **D'Arros** and neighbouring **St Joseph Atoll** are privately owned and also out of bounds above the high tide mark, though charter boats visit St Joseph for the excellent fly-fishing opportunities of the lagoon. There is a small settlement on **Poivre Atoll** and it is possible to land here in good conditions via a small boat channel. **Marie Louise** is also inhabited, but remains covered in nesting seabirds. Landing is very difficult except in the calmest

Aerial view of St Joseph Atoll

conditions. There are also large seabird colonies at the protected islands of **Etoile** and **Boudeuse**, and at **Desnoeufs**, where sooty tern eggs are collected for consumption by the Seychelles populace, but landing at all three islands is extremely difficult except in the calmest conditions.

ALDABRA AND THE SOUTHERN ATOLLS

The World Heritage Site of **Aldabra** ⓴ is difficult to reach, being 1,150km (700 miles) southwest of Mahé. However, for the determined few, a visit will be the main purpose of their Seychelles holiday. A live-aboard vessel, Sea Star, offer regular scheduled trips, either sailing to/from Mahé or flying to Assumption 40km (25 miles) south of Aldabra to join the vessel. Some charter boats can arrange tailor-made trips.

Aldabra is the Galapagos of the Indian Ocean. It has the world's largest population of giant tortoises (about 100,000), the last surviving flightless bird of the region (the Aldabra rail), one

ECOTOURISM

Ecotourism is at the heart of tourism in the Seychelles for a reason. If you want a simple beach holiday, there are many cheaper alternatives, but the Seychelles has seized upon its one big competitive advantage. It can offer something beyond price: a glimpse of Eden.

To be an ecotourist in the Seychelles, you do not need to be a telescope-toting twitcher. You just need to have a sense of appreciation of the natural beauty of islands, the intense colours of the tropics, the proliferation of nature and the relatively pristine environment that is the Seychelles. If beaches are your thing, then the islands can offer the best in the world, as testified by many a survey. Beyond the beach is a relatively unspoilt environment, with nearly half the landmass protected in one form or another. Just about every endemic bird is increasing in numbers. So are tortoises and turtles. The Seychelles has pioneered whale shark protection in the Indian Ocean.

Ecotourism has given the environment an economic value that hopefully ensures its future. In contrast to some depressing TV documentaries full of gloom and doom, here is the other side of the coin.

of the world's largest frigate bird colonies (10,000 pairs) and a wealth of endemic flora and fauna. It is the world's largest raised coral atoll. It forms a third of the landmass of the Seychelles, with 46 islands, uninhabited except for the small Research Station on Picard. Diving is excellent and exciting in the channels into the massive lagoon.

Cosmoledo Atoll is an overnight run by boat from Aldabra. It is totally uninhabited except for wildlife, including huge colonies of boobies of three different species. Diving is generally even better than

Giant Tortoise on Aldabra atoll

at Aldabra. Best of all for diving is the wall of Astove Atoll, while ashore the ruins of the former settlement and the cemetery are poignant reminders of people who either tried to make a living on this remote outpost or were shipwrecked and drowned.

The ten islands of **Farquhar Atoll** lie 770km (480 miles) south-southwest of Mahé. Here there is a settlement where copra is produced in small quantities and an airstrip on **North Island**. Many of the trees of **South Island** have been turned white by the droppings of seabirds. Beyond this, **Goëlettes** is the most southerly island of Seychelles, a wild, windswept place with huge numbers of nesting terns. Fly-fishing for bonefish and giant trevally is excellent, and it is often possible to fly from Mahé to stay on a live-aboard vessel. There are some small five-star villas on North Island.

WHAT TO DO

SPORTS AND OUTDOOR PURSUITS

Most activities in the Seychelles revolve around the sea and there is a good range of watersports available. Away from the beach there are mountains and some excellent walks. The Seychelles has some of the most pristine tropical islands in the world and is a nature lover's paradise. Birdwatching is excellent, not just on the nature reserve islands but on the main islands too. Horse-riding and golf can also be enjoyed in beautiful surroundings.

WATERSPORTS

Conditions are generally excellent all year round for watersports, though occasionally there is either too much wind for beginners or too little for the experienced. All the larger hotels offer activities, including windsurfing, canoeing, hobiecats and water-skiing. Beau Vallon on Mahé and Cote d'Or on Praslin are the main centres, and equipment is available to hire (including to non-residents of the hotels). Leisure 2000 (open daily 10am–5pm, tel: 248-259 4367) at Beau Vallon offers lessons for novices in both motorised and non-motorised watersports and also paragliding. Body and board surfing is good on beaches exposed to onshore winds, but care should be taken of currents and undertows.

DIVING

Diving in the Seychelles is superb, particularly during the calm periods of March–April and mid-October–mid-December when visibility is best. The variety of fish life is stunning, as is the underwater scenery, including the topography of the granitic islands and the steep walls of the outer islands. Corals

Woman snorkelling off Cousine Island

are a little disappointing, still recovering from the exceptional coral bleaching of 1998, when prolonged sea temperatures wiped out 95 percent of reefs in the granitics.

Underwater Centre (open daily 8.30am–5pm, tel: 248-4345 445; www.diveseychelles.com.sc) operates top-class dive centres offering the full range of PADI courses at Coral Strand and Beau Vallon Beach Resort. Fully equipped power catamarans load directly from the beach, with one boat dedicated to longer-range dive sites for up to eight, including the best opportunities to dive with whale sharks. On Praslin, Octopus Divers (open daily 8.30am–5pm, tel: 248-423 2602; www.octopusdiver.com) is the longest-established dive centre and operates dives from Berjaya Praslin Beach Hotel. One-day introductory courses are available weekdays and should be booked at least a day in advance. All major dive centres have dive and snorkelling equipment for hire.

Dive sites on the inner islands vary in depth from 8–30m (26–100ft). Inshore dives in the granitics are more sheltered, shallower sites, ideal for beginners. Offshore dive sites of the granitics, and all diving in the outer islands, are more suitable for experienced divers as these tend to be deeper and may have currents. Live-aboard dive trips can be arranged to more remote destinations.

In the granitic islands, the main attractions are the numbers and variety of colourful reef fish and the underwater scenery with huge boulders and narrow caves. In the outer islands, ocean-going fish are more prolific and the scenery different, often with steep atoll walls decorated with beautiful gorgonian fan corals.

Shark Watch

The Seychelles is a great place to spot whale sharks. Surveys have located as many as 49 in a single day. This is the world's biggest fish, reaching 15m (50ft) or more in length.

Snorkelling with whale sharks

GLASS-BOTTOM BOAT

A glass-bottom boat trip is the ideal way to see the reef without getting your feet wet. On Mahé, tour operators offer trips to St Anne Marine National Park with lunch on one of the small islands (Moyenne, Round or Cerf). You may also transfer to a sub-sea viewer – a semi-submersible boat that affords a horizontal view of the reef, thereby scaring fewer fish than the glass-bottom boat. St Anne Marine Park is not as good as it used to be, but it is still a good introduction to the coral reef.

Teddy's Glass Bottom Boat (open daily, tel: 248-2511198) operates out of Coral Strand Hotel, Beau Vallon, taking visitors to Baie Ternay National Marine Park on the west coast, where soft corals abound. The trip to the park past the dramatic cliffs and granite boulders adds to the enjoyment.

WALKING

There are some wild and atmospheric places to be explored in the Seychelles. The best time for walking is from May to

October when paths are drier and humidity lower. Several walks have yellow trail markers so it is not essential to have a guide. You can pick up excellent, inexpensive trail guides produced by the Ministry of Environment from bookshops and tourism outlets. Guided walks are also available.

There are several walks in Morne Seychellois National Park on Mahé. The cliffs above Victoria, known as Trois Frères, can be reached in about half an hour via an 800 metre (1/2 mile) walk, climbing 200m (660ft) altitude. The main feature is the panoramic view of Victoria and beyond to the islands. Morne Blanc is a 1km (1/2 mile) steep walk through mist forest to the summit with a spectacular vertical drop and magnificent views on clear days. Copolia is a little more difficult, particularly towards the top, and though only 1.2km (3/4 mile) in length, a good hour and a half should be allowed. This is the best mountain trail for the enthusiast, with the contrasting ecology of the forest and

Hiking in the heart of the Morne Seychellois National Park

the glacis (exposed granite), dominated by insectivorous pitcher plants, screwpines and endemic sedges.

There is an easier but longer Mahé walk along the coast from Danzil to Anse Major, skirting the park. Anse Major can only be reached on foot, so it is often possible to have the picturesque little bay to yourself. It is excellent for

Creole guide with machete, La Digue

swimming, and snorkelling around the rocks is good.

On Praslin, Jean Baptiste Nature Trail (behind Coco de Mer hotel) is rich in endemic flora and fauna. A map and trail guide can be purchased from the hotel. There is also a walk at Glacis Noir, Praslin National Park (a short distance uphill from the Vallée de Mai entrance), excellent for panoramas and to see black parrots. The more energetic might try the Zimbabwe to Anse Lazio trail, allowing 4–5 hours.

Silhouette, with no roads, is excellent for walking. There are easy walks along the coast from La Passe in either direction, and more difficult but rewarding walks into the mountains. One of these leads from La Passe to the summit of Mont Pot à Eau. This should not be attempted without a guide as the path is unclear and often muddy and slippery due to high rainfall. A full day trip is required, and the Nature Protection Trust of Seychelles can provide a guide if booked in advance (tel: 248-323711).

GOLF

There is one 18-hole golf course in the Seychelles at Lemuria Resort (tel: 4282281) on Praslin. The par-70 course is a challenging one, particularly from the 13th hole onward, where it departs from the flat coastal plateau to climb the adjacent steep slopes. Pools, bunkers and the topography of the land provide a series of challenges. The par-five 18th hole is particularly inspiring, the elevated tee shot offering a remarkable view of the green, a large lake, and beyond to the clubhouse and the Indian Ocean.

On Mahé, Seychelles Golf Club (tel: 2781902) is a 9-hole golf course at Anse aux Pins, 1km (1/2 mile) south of the end of the airport. Any visiting golfer with a handicap wishing to enjoy a round or participate in competitions (Thur and Sat) is welcome. Advance booking is not necessary except for the Saturday Competition (bring your handicap card), which you should book by Thursday 6pm. It is an attractive course in an old coconut plantation, kinder to golfers who slice than those that hook, the latter often ending up in the swamp. The best time to play is when it is cooler, from around 8.30am or after 3.30pm.

CRUISING

Taking a live-aboard boat means you take your hotel room with you, all your transfer costs are included, and, if the boat is skippered, many of the transits can be done while you relax. For much of the year, wind speeds are ideal, in the range of force 2–5. During the strongest winds of May to September, the sea between Mahé and other islands is rough, but there are still many sheltered anchorages. The Seychelles is outside the cyclone belt, but squalls can be experienced from December to February. Moorings are available at Marine National Parks and nature reserves, where a small fee is charged for entry. Larger charter boats carry full dive equipment and may provide a dive master. Most vessels will at least have snorkelling equipment, and almost all will carry fishing tackle.

Silhouette Cruises (tel: 248-4324026; www.seychelles-cruises.com) offers larger vessels accommodating up to 16 guests with 8 crew. *Sea Shell* and *Sea Pearl* are traditional twin-masted top-sail schooners, built in Holland a century ago. *Sea Star* is more modern and spacious, with nine cabins, all en suite. For most of the year they make scheduled weekly cruises through the granitic islands. They are also available for full boat tailor-made charters as far afield as Aldabra.

Small, fast motor-cruisers for those who wish to minimise transit times may be chartered through Waterworld (tel: 248-2514735). Boats are available for up to 10 passengers on 3-day, 6-day or tailor-made packages.

Several companies have catamarans or monohulls for bareboat, skippered or fully-crewed charters. Most offer a provisioning service, very useful to save time. The majority of boats are 11–15 metres (37–50ft) for up to eight passengers.

The green at Lemuria Golf Course, Lemuria Resort

Catamaran near St. Pierre Island

No official qualifications or licences are required for bareboat charter but at least one member of your party should have good sailing experience. On Mahé, companies include Sunsail at the Eden Island Marina (tel: 248-4346 122; www.sunsail.com), Moorings at Wharf Hotel (www.moorings.com) and Angel Fish Ltd. (tel: 4344644; www.seychelles-charter.com).

On Praslin, Dream Yacht Seychelles (tel: 4232681; www.dream-yacht-seychelles.com) offers overnight charters, which may also be bareboat, skippered or fully-crewed on catamarans of up to 25 metre (82ft). Standard itineraries are 6 or 10 nights around the granitics, extending to the Amirantes in calm seas.

SCENIC FLIGHTS

Helicopter Seychelles (tel: 4385858; www.helicopterseychelles.com) take scenic flights around Mahé, Praslin or La Digue and the adjacent islands, an excellent way to see the contrasting colours of the Seychelles: the greens of the forest, the azures of the sea, the dark granite cliffs and dazzling white coral sands. Flights last 15, 30, 45 or 60 minutes. There are four seats, one by the pilot and three behind. The front seat is best for an all-round view, but photographers may prefer a back window seat, where slots slide open for cameras. There is a small slot at the front but it is lower and difficult to use.

FISHING

Game fishing and bottom fishing are good all year round, though the unsettled peak of the rainy season, from mid-December to January is best avoided. January to March is best for kingfish or wahoo, August to December for sailfish and November to December for *karang* or trevally. Tuna, dorado and bonito can be taken year round. Marlin is occasionally taken. Bottom fishing for red snapper (or *bourzwa*) and green jobfish *(zob)* can be arranged, including night trips departing 5pm and returning after midnight. Many power boats and yachts are available for charter by the day or longer. Reservations may be made at local agents or through The Marine Charter Association, Victoria, Mahé (tel: 4322 126).

Some atolls of the outer islands offer superb fly-fishing, notably St François and St Joseph Atolls from mid-September to mid-May. Charters to the more remote atolls of Farquhar, Astove and Cosmoledo can also be arranged. Bonefishing is probably the best in the world. Other fish taken regularly on the fly include five species of trevally, three triggerfish and more. The record from St Francois is 42 different species in a single week. The greatest challenge of all to the fly-fisherman is milkfish, likened to the marine equivalent of a 4.2-litre Porsche. Once thought to be

Deep sea fishing

Red Fody on Praslin

impossible to catch on flies, a technique to catch milkfish was pioneered at Alphonse.

BIRDWATCHING

The Seychelles is special for birdwatchers because of its unique land birds (12 endemics), spectacular seabird colonies and rare migrants. A visit to Cousin or Aride is a must for anyone who wants to see a truly pristine island, free of introduced predators. For the real enthusiast, a full day on Aride offers more than a shorter guided tour of Cousin, but Cousin is more accessible year-round. On Mahé, the mudflats of Victoria and Providence are excellent for waders, while scops owls and white-eyes can be found in the mountains. Praslin has its black parrot and La Digue the beautiful paradise flycatcher. Bird Island is the best island for rare migrants. The Seychelles Bird Records Committee has recorded 240 species and encourages visitors to report interesting sightings on their website at www.stokecoll.ac.uk/sbrc.

HORSE RIDING

Utegangar Riding Center, Barbarons, Mahé (tel: 248-712355), takes bookings at least 24 hours in advance. Riding hats are provided and a junior saddle is available, and you must wear long trousers and closed sports shoes. Most riding is on Barbarons or Grand Anse beaches, usually at low tide; inexperienced riders are usually led or accompanied. Most rides are 1–2 hours, with longer 3–5 hour excursions into the mountains including a refreshing break at the Grand Anse waterfall. Horse riding is also available at L'Union Estate, La Digue.

SHOPPING

Do not expect exclusive upmarket boutiques or bargain prices, and even some of the souvenirs that are available may disappoint, being imported from Madagascar, Africa or elsewhere. Victoria has the greatest choice, with many kiosks and souvenir shops. Here you will find brightly coloured beach wraps, T-shirts, beachwear, shell jewellery, coconut crafts and other cheaper goods, most of which are locally made. More expensive and lasting souvenirs are available at Memorabilia on Revolution Avenue and Sunstroke on Market Street, including fine hand-embroidered linen, hand-made clothing, mobiles, mirrors and lampshades. The Craft Centre

Colourful Market Street in Victoria

at Anse aux Pins, with basketware and other locally made products, is also worth visiting.

For something more unusual, and truly Seychellois, why not take home a bottle of liqueur made from local ingredients, or a handful of cinnamon quills, a bottle of lemongrass oil (an excellent mosquito deterrent and a refreshing perfume), a bottle crammed with red hot chillies – known as 'Hellfire', or a local *fatak* (soft grass) or *zig* broom (used to sweep outdoors), all of which are available from the Seychelles market. Local tea, grown without chemicals in a pollution-free atmosphere, is marketed as the 'purest organic tea on earth'. It is available in a range of flavours

THE MOUTYA

The traditional Seychelles *moutya* is more an event than a dance. In the dark days of slavery it was one way the slaves could express themselves. In a clearing in the forest they lit a fire and sat whilst musicians tuned their drums, tightening the skins in the heat of the flames. When they struck up a rhythm the couples stood to dance. The 'step' is merely a sideways shuffle and a sway of the hips. The couples do not touch, having the contradictory effect of making the mood more sensual. Audience members stood to call out a sing-song commentary in time to the beat; an early form of rapping. It is often a funny or ribald story, making fun of a well-known local character. In slave times the subject might be one of the plantation owners, or the chant would be a lament for lost homes and loved ones. The evening sometimes ended with romantic liaisons in the woods, and this scandalised the colonial authorities so much they attempted to outlaw the dance, but it can still be seen today, often in special performances for tourists, and should not be missed.

including vanilla and lemon.
Visit the studios of local artists for prints and original
works including watercol-
ours, oils and batiks (just
be prepared – they're not
cheap). The ultimate sou-
venir however, is a home-
grown black pearl from
Praslin, mounted in an
exquisite pendant.

NIGHTLIFE

Nobody comes to the Sey-
chelles for its nightlife, and
indeed the whole ethos of
a holiday here is escape
and peace and quiet. The
larger hotels on Mahé and
Praslin will have live local

*Berjaya Beau Vallon
Resort & Casino*

bands a few nights of the week, and even many of the
smaller ones will have a local singer to entertain dinner
guests. Traditional *moutya* evenings may also be organised.
On Mahé there is also a cinema, although films are not
exactly up to date. On Praslin, Jungle Disco, Grande Anse
(tel: 512683) offers local and international music Friday and
Saturday 10pm–4am. There are three bars and a pool room,
and snacks are available.

  Mahé has two casinos; Casino des Seychelles at Beau
Vallon Bay Hotel (open daily 7pm–3am, tel: 4287287) offers
free transport to and from most Mahé hotels. Berjaya Beau
Vallon Resort and Casino (open 8pm–2am, tel: 4286286;
www.berjayahotel.com) is more sophisticated and offers

Boy playing on beach

free transport from west-coast hotels. Casino des Isles at Cote d'Or, Praslin (open Mon–Sat 7.30pm–3am, slots daily noon–2am, tel: 4232500; www.casinocity.sc) is housed in the same imposing building as the excellent restaurant Tante Mimi.

CHILDREN'S SEYCHELLES

Children who love being on the beach and in the sea all day long will love the Seychelles; those who like constant entertainment and organised activities most probably will not. Older children will enjoy learning to snorkel and dive. The Seychelles is also a very safe destination for babies, with high hygiene standards and an absence of major diseases.

A few of the larger hotels operate clubs for children, but there are no talent shows, amusement parks or any of the children's activities arranged at resorts elsewhere. Apart from a few exclusive hotels which specifically exclude children below a certain age, children will be made welcome everywhere.

The Seychellois are relaxed with children, although children are expected to be well behaved. Overall, the Seychelles is a safe place for children, although you should bear in mind the usual dangers associated with the sea, boats, heat and strong sunshine. The smaller islands offer them the chance for exploration and adventure, a rarity in this day and age.

CALENDAR OF EVENTS

March, May, October SUBIOS, annual underwater festival. Famous names from the world of underwater photography visit the Seychelles as guests of the Tourist Board. Film shows and presentations take place at many of the major hotels. There are photography competitions and other marine-related events. The date varies each year. See www.subios.com for more details.

April Rotary Annual Fishing Tournament; a 3-day tournament for trolling and bottom fishing. Mainly an event for local boat owners, but visitors are welcome to join in. Details available from Marine Charter Association (tel: 4322126).

April–May Seychelles Art Festival. Exhibitions by local artists and local and international music performances, Victoria.

June Agricultural and Horticultural Show, Mahé. A 3-day event showcasing competitive and non-competitive agricultural displays and exhibits organised by the Ministry of Agriculture & Marine Resources (tel: 4378252).

July Round Table Annual Regatta, Mahé. A two-day weekend event at Beau Vallon with games and sporting events on land and at sea. The boating community gathers offshore, and onshore it is party time.

15 August Feast of the Assumption of the Virgin Mary/La Digue Festival. A big day for La Diguois, when the island is lively and crowded with various land-based events, stalls and competitions. Many boats are chartered to visit La Digue for the weekend, and the atmosphere of this normally sleepy island is transformed.

September Festival Creole. The biggest event of the Seychelles' cultural calendar, celebrating Creole traditions with a week of shows, displays and music. Musicians and performers from other countries of the Creole world come to the Seychelles to take part.

September–October Mahé–Praslin Windsurfing Race. Race starts from Victoria Harbour and is open to all. Conditions are perfect at this time of year, with fairly strong winds blowing from the southeast. Contact the Seychelles Yachting Association for details (tel: 4722328).

EATING OUT

In the early evening the air in the Seychelles is filled with the fragrant smell of garlic and spices cooking. The Seychellois do not keep Mediterranean hours for meals as they do in many hot countries. They usually breakfast early, take lunch between midday and two, and eat dinner early also; a habit retained from the days when you needed to prepare your food before it went dark and there was no electricity. Breakfast is much as you may have at home, perhaps with more exotic fruits on offer, such as pawpaw, guava and mango. Some Seychellois have fond childhood memories of starting the day with a breakfast of tinned, sweetened condensed milk spread on a sandwich, but this is unlikely to be offered in your hotel.

A Seychellois lunch is fairly typical of the modern-day diet and tends to be a sandwich, takeaway; or it may be skipped entirely. The evening meal is the big event of the day. In fact many restaurants away from the beaches only open in the evenings. Some restaurants will be open and busy by 6.30pm, but the usual opening time is 7pm and many restaurants will be closed by 10pm or 10.30pm. Restaurants in hotels may start and finish a little later.

There is not a wide range in the quality of food offered by restaurants; it is all pretty good, but you will find it expensive, especially if you order wine or other alcoholic drinks. What varies is the service and the 'frills'. Some of the best

Save the Turtles

When the sea was too rough for fishing, the Seychellois relied upon alternative sources of protein: green turtle, tortoise and seabirds' eggs, none of which is widely available today due to conservation legislation. A young giant tortoise was traditionally bought upon the birth of a daughter and eaten at her wedding feast.

Grilled goatfish at Lanbousir Restaurant, La Digue

food can be found in the most unprepossessing surroundings, and even in the smallest takeaway outlet, hygiene
standards are usually good. You should have no difficulty
with the menus, which will either be in English or French
with a translation. A few of the specialist terms you may be
unfamiliar with are explained here. Self-caterers will need
to explore the many local shops where most owners are
friendly and helpful. Useful basics include locally produced
ham and bacon, which will be fattier than you are used to,
but very tasty.

As a general rule, you will find better bread in dedicated
bakeries in Victoria than in local shops. Vegetables may not
look as clean or regular as they are at home, but they taste
fine. You will find meat in chest freezers in almost every
shop. Again, it is not particularly well presented, but is of
reasonable quality and is kept more deeply frozen than produce in Europe for food hygiene reasons.

Barbecue on the beach

FISH AND SEAFOOD

It comes as no surprise that the speciality of the Seychelles is fish. Surrounded by thousands of miles of ocean, the Seychellois have always had access to the very freshest and most flavoursome fish and they make the most of it in a variety of ways, from simple, meaty barbecued tuna steaks to hot and exotic fish curries. Although the cooking style is generally referred to as 'Creole', the Seychelles cuisine is unique, differing from that of nearby Mauritius, and benefits from the influence of the French, Chinese, the Indians and even the British who introduced fish and chips – though the fish is of course usually the more exotic parrotfish *(kakatwa)* and not cod.

Most of the better restaurants take a more sophisticated and subtle slant on their use of fish and the Seychelles has to be one of the best places in the world to try raw fish (usually sailfish or swordfish) dressed with lime or smoked sailfish as a starter. Another unusual dish you may come across is shark chutney or *satini*, shark meat grated and cooked with turmeric and *bilimbi*, a sour fruit similar to a tiny cucumber. *Bourzwa*, sometimes spelled the French way, *bourgeois*, is red snapper. This is a white fleshed fish, especially prized for grilling whole over hot coals, stuffed with garlic, tomatoes, onions and chillies, regularly basted with fresh lime juice. Whole fish such as mackerel are often served this way. If you are squeamish, be warned that a grilled fish *(pwason grille)* will usually be served unfilleted, with head and tail on.

Seafood features on most menus; enjoy wonderful local prawns and crab (the lobster is usually imported) as well as two local shellfish species: the *palourd* (a small clam), often served in garlic butter and the *tektek* (a smaller clam), usually made into a soup which will probably come with the shells in it.

MEAT

If you are not a fish and seafood lover, there is no need to worry. There will always be meat dishes on the menu in the Seychelles. Chicken, beef, mutton, pork and occasionally goat feature widely, as does the spicy local sausage which

HOW TO COOK OCTOPUS

Local chefs excel at achieving a melt-in-the-mouth texture when they cook octopus. Far from a fiercely guarded secret handed down through the generations, the reality is much more banal.

The first stage in the process could not be simpler. Having caught your octopus and gutted it, removing the beak and ink sacks (a messy but vital job), you should then bash it; drape it over a rock and hit it repeatedly with a stick. It is then ready for the next step, and here the method becomes somewhat hazy. Some say the secret of softening octopus is to boil it with a wine bottle cork (perhaps a Creole joke), while others suggest to cook it with a piece of pawpaw. Pawpaw contains a digestive enzyme which breaks down the protein in the flesh, thus softening it. The most popular method is no real secret at all though, it's simply to use a pressure cooker...

is traditionally cooked with lentils in a stew. The quality of imported beef is generally good, though the local pork, especially that used in many of the curries, can be rather fatty. You will get chicken breast fillet in the more upmarket restaurants. Takeaways offer more robust, everyday dishes, and the quality of the meat may be slightly lower but naturally, you get what you pay for. Staples commonly found in these outlets include a variety of stews and curries. In the cheaper venues, chicken is usually cubed but not cut off the bone and tends to consist of the least meaty parts, making a chicken curry a bit of a challenge to eat.

HOT STUFF

Local curries are decidedly hot, though in restaurants frequented by tourists they will be much milder. There is something unique about a Seychelles curry which makes it slightly

Chicken coconut curry - a local speciality

different to the better-known Indian dish. With local chillies, the smaller they are the bigger the punch they pack. A small dish of minced chillies in oil or vinegar is often served with a meal and should be approached with caution - a little goes a long way! One speciality curry well worth trying is the *kari koko*, made with coconut milk. Octopus is often prepared in this way, and it also works well with

Market goods in Victoria

chicken. They have a knack for preparing octopus here so that it almost melts in the mouth. Curries, like most dishes, are served with plain white rice, salad and chutneys. These refreshing side dishes consist of raw, grated green pawpaw, mango, golden apple or carrot with finely chopped onion, dressed with lime juice and pepper, and they make the ideal accompaniment to a fiery curry.

VEGETABLES

There is not a huge variety of vegetables available, but local specialities include aubergine fritters, thin slices of aubergine deep fried in light batter, the peppery local watercress, a variety of *breds* (any sort of green leafy vegetable such as Chinese cabbage, or *bred mouroung*, the leaves of the locally grown horseradish tree), besides the more conventional carrots or potatoes. If you have enjoyed your visit to the Seychelles then be sure to eat breadfruit before you leave. Tradition has it that if you do, you are sure to return.

Tropical fruit for sale

It is delicious cooked the traditional way; slowly baked in a fire pit and served simply with butter and salt as you would a baked potato, but locally it is also used to make chips and crisps. The living shoot of one of the endemic palms used to be served as *palmiste* or Millionaire's Salad (to obtain it, the whole tree had to be felled), but as these plants are now protected, the soft inner core of the common coconut palm is used as a most acceptable substitute. It is usually prepared with a light lime juice dressing as a starter or in cheese sauce for a more substantial dish.

DESSERTS

Unless you are a great fruit lover there is no need to save much room for dessert, which will usually be a choice between ice cream, sorbet or fruit salad. However, exotic fruits such as jamalac, guava, mango and passion fruit will feature and are served with coconut milk instead of cream. Sometimes fruit salad is served with nougat or caramelised coconut. Ice creams and sorbets are locally made and are very good. More unusual flavours on offer include coconut and lemon grass.

An authentic local dessert is the *daube*, a stodgy pudding consisting of banana or breadfruit simmered in coconut milk, but you do not often see this on menus. Hotels may have a bit more variety on the desserts trolley compared to local restaurants.

WHAT TO DRINK

To wash your curry down you could drink one of the excellent local lager beers (Seybrew and Eku), or a Guinness, also brewed under licence in the Seychelles. There are various fruit juices available, most delicious when freshly squeezed. Visitors are often surprised by how delicious and refreshing a glass of fresh lime can be, subtly flavoured with salt and sugar, and you will probably at some point be offered a *kokotann* (green coconut) with the top removed so that you can drink the coconut water within.

You will find bottled water available everywhere, and it is handy to keep some with you to prevent dehydration, but the tap water is also quite safe to drink, if somewhat heavy on chlorine. Do not drink water from the streams - it may look crystal clear but you have no way of knowing what goes on upstream.

Wine and all alcoholic drinks are imported and come with a large mark-up

Coconut Milk

To make coconut milk, scrape out the white flesh of a coconut and put the pieces into a bowl. Soak with water (or milk for extra creaminess), cover and leave in a cool place overnight. In the morning you'll have a layer of coconut milk, and a topping of coconut cream. Strain before use.

in all hotels and restaurants. The truly local brews are not widely available but they are *kalou* (palm toddy), *baka* (fermented sugar-cane juice – *not* rum!), and *lapire*, a fiery brew basically made of anything that will ferment when sugar is added. These are all heady brews and they should be sampled in moderation.

Instant coffee in the Seychelles can be rather disappointing but the filter coffee is usually good. Local tea, which is organically grown in the mountains, is pleasant and delicate, if not particularly strong. Other blends of tea are not widely available although you will find vanilla tea, which is made from locally grown tea that has been subtly flavoured with vanilla pods.

An excellent alternative way to round off your meal is with a cup of *sitronel* (from the French *citronelle*) or lemongrass tea, which is refreshing and reputed to aid digestion.

High tea at Glacis Cerf, Frégate Island resort

PLACES TO EAT

Restaurants do not stay open as late as in some other holiday resorts. There is a 15 percent Value Added Tax. If this is not included in prices on the menu, then this will be stated. The following approximate guide indicates prices for a three-course meal (or for a two-course meal where three courses are not available) for one person with drinks:

€€€€ over 70 euros   **€€€** 40–70 euros
€€ 25–40 euros   **€** below 25 euros

MAHÉ

VICTORIA

George Camille Art Gallery (Kaz Zanana) €€ *Revolution Avenue, tel: 4324150.* An attractive old restored wooden house on the edge of town, ideal for a light lunch or toasted sandwich, but save room for the excellent cakes and creamy cappuccino. Worth a visit to see the mini art gallery featuring the colourful work of local artist George Camille.

Marie Antoinette €€ *Serret Road, tel: 4266222.* At the foot of Signal Hill above Victoria, this is the best place to sample a broad range of Creole cuisine. No choice is offered for the main course, but a large number of dishes are brought to the table, featuring tuna, parrotfish, bourgeois (red snapper), chicken curry, fish stew, aubergine fritters and local vegetables. Dessert is less imaginative, but by then you'll probably be full anyway!

Rendezvous €€€ *Victoria House, Francis Rachel Street, tel: 4323556.* On a veranda overlooking the clock tower, this is the place for a more substantial meal than the light meals offered elsewhere around town. Very popular at lunchtime with the local business community, but quieter in the evenings.

Sam's Pizzeria €€ *Francis Rachel Street, tel: 4344299.* Excellent pizzas and a lot more besides are offered on the extensive menu at this restaurant. Simple, good-quality cooking with a minimum of fuss. Open lunchtime and evenings. If you are in a hurry, the takeaway downstairs is good, though it gets very busy and the speed of service is not the same as a Western fast-food takeaway.

NORTH MAHÉ

Baobab Pizzeria € *Beau Vallon, tel: 4247167.* A very popular cheap and cheerful restaurant, with stone benches and a sandy floor that merges with the beach. Pizzas are the speciality, but the pasta dishes and fish and chips are also good. It is usually difficult to get a table after 7pm until the early birds relinquish their seats for the second sitting.

Boat House €€ *Beau Vallon, tel: 4247898;* www.boathousesey chelles.com. Eat as much as you like at an excellent evening fish barbecue with a huge array of local dishes on offer. It is essential to book in advance at this very popular venue and to be there by 7.30pm if possible, when the buffet begins.

Coco D'Or €€ *Beau Vallon, tel: 4247331;* www.cocodor.sc. This small hotel inland from the beach has two excellent cheap and cheerful restaurants, one Chinese and one pizzeria, in addition to the main restaurant used by the hotel guests. The Chinese restaurant in particular is top quality and excellent value for money. It is air-conditioned, which is very pleasant on humid evenings. Open daily.

La Scala €€€€ *Bel Ombre, tel: 4247535.* This Italian-run upmarket restaurant is the number-one choice with the local business community for evening entertaining, so booking is essential. When the locals rate it so highly, you know it has to be good! Evenings only, closed Sundays.

Le Corsaire €€€€ *Bel Ombre, tel: 4247171.* Housed in a wonderful stone-and-thatch building right on the shoreline, offering quality international (with an Italian flavour) and upmarket Creole cuisine. Evenings only, closed Monday.

Mahék Restaurant €€ *Coral Strand Hotel, Beau Vallon, tel: 4291000.* The only choice for an Indian meal. A large range of authentic dishes is offered, with a choice of mild, medium or hot, according to taste. Air-conditioned right next to the beach. Open lunch and dinner from 7pm, closed Tuesdays.

Perle Noire €€€€ *Beau Vallon, tel: 4620220*. Set back from the beach, a short stroll from Coral Strand Hotel, this is an excellent restaurant serving good steaks as well as imaginative fish and seafood dishes.

SOUTH MAHÉ

Anchor Café € *Anse à la Mouche, tel: 4371289*. The Anchor Café makes a good lunchtime stopping-off point when on an island tour of Mahé. The café offers light snacks in a garden setting opposite the beach.

Chez Plume €€€ *Anse Boileau, tel: 4355050*. The emphasis is on seafood at this excellent restaurant, but meat is also available. Unlike most venues, the desserts are superb, particularly the extravagant passion fruit soufflé.

Jardin du Roi €€ *Anse Royale, tel: 4371313*. Set in the tranquil surroundings of the spice garden, the small restaurant serves good food at reasonable prices. The ice creams are particularly interesting, with exotic flavours such as cinnamon and lemon grass. Curry buffet every Sunday, when booking is advisable.

Kaz Kreol €€ *Anse Royale, tel: 4371680*. A wonderful casual setting, right on the beach, offering a variety of meals from pizzas to Chinese to International. Ideal for a stop on an island tour.

Vye Marmit €€€ *Anse aux Pins, tel: 4376155*. In the grounds of the Craft Village, the restaurant is on a large veranda of a traditional plantation building. Creole cuisine is the speciality, but there are one or two meat dishes on offer too.

PRASLIN

Bonbon Plume €€€ *Anse Lazio, tel: 4232136*. Mainly French cooking, right by one of the most beautiful beaches in the world, served at wooden tables shaded by palm-thatched umbrellas.

Britannia Restaurant €€ *Grand Anse, tel: 4233215.* The Britannia is a pleasant, relaxing venue, especially at lunchtime when, with a bit of luck, black parrots may come to the garden to feed in the fruit trees.

La Gouloue Cafe €€ *Côte d'Or, tel: 4232223.* A small, quiet restaurant set back from the beach, offering tasty snacks to keep you going through the day.

La Pirogue €€ *Anse Volbert, tel: 4236677.* A nice café-restaurant serving international meals with variety of salads and a generous selection of fish and meat dishes, as well as vegetarian options.

Les Rochers €€€€ *La Pointe, tel: 4233910.* On the beach, an excellent restaurant specialising in seafood and fish dishes. Tues–Sat evenings only.

Tante Mimi €€€€ *Anse Volbert, tel: 4232500.* An unusual imposing building houses the only Casino and an exceptionally good restaurant, itself with interesting decor. While on Praslin, it is well worth a visit for that special meal out. In the evenings, the restaurant will arrange collection and return to any Praslin hotel. International and Creole cuisine; evenings only but lunch is offered on Sundays.

Vanille Restaurant €€ *Anse La Blague, tel: 4232178.* Simple but very good Creole cuisine in relaxed surroundings on a terrace overlooking the waters of one of the quietest corners of Praslin.

LA DIGUE

Loutier Coco Bar & Restaurant €€ *Grand Anse.* Bar open daily 9am–5pm, with a Creole buffet 12.30–2.30pm. Open evenings upon demand. Excellent food in a very picturesque beach-side setting.

Zerof Bar & Restaurant € *tel: 4 234439.* Situated opposite the Flycatcher Reserve. Open all day every day, so it's ideal for the self-caterer who has a change of heart! Cheap and cheerful Creole cuisine.

A–Z TRAVEL TIPS

A Summary of Practical Information

A

ACCOMMODATION (see also Camping, Youth Hostels, and the list of Recommended Hotels on page 132)

Accommodation ranges across a broad spectrum from small guesthouses and self-catering to fairly big hotels, but in recent years there has been a strong move towards the 5-star market. Almost all accommodation is expensive by international standards. There are no high-rise hotels. Indeed, there are few that exceed two storeys. Many hotels offer good discounts if booked direct online. Rates are higher during peak periods which coincide with holidays in Europe around Christmas/New Year, Easter and July/August.

Most accommodation and the greatest variety are on Mahé and Praslin, with a lesser number of places to stay on La Digue. This includes all large hotels, self-catering establishments and guesthouses. Hotels on coral islands and small granitic islands tend to be around 30 rooms in size, a few even smaller. If opting for self-catering, bear in mind that food choices will be more limited than you are used to; even some basic items run out from time to time and ready meals are not easy to find.

AIRPORT

Seychelles **International Airport on Mahé** is 10km (6 miles) south of Victoria. There is a tourism information desk before Immigration and a duty-free shop in the Arrivals hall. Beyond customs there are car hire, bank facilities and tour operator desks and, beyond these, the taxi rank. Those who have booked through a tour operator will be greeted immediately upon exiting Customs and escorted to the appropriate minibus for transfer to hotels. There is a petrol station and bus stop immediately opposite the airport. If connecting to a flight to Praslin or another island, turn right after exiting Customs and proceed past the check-in desks and restaurant, following the covered walkway round to the Domestic Terminal. Helicopter Seychelles uses this same terminal for flights and has its own desk.

B

BICYCLE HIRE

Bicycles are the main form of transport for visitors to La Digue, where there are several bicycle hire outlets close to the jetty at La Passe, including Chez Michelin, next to the Post Office. Cycling is also available on Praslin through some hotels (for residents only) or at Cote d'Or, next to Praslin Beach Hotel.

On some of the small islands such as Alphonse and Desroches, every guest is provided with a bicycle for their private use. The topography of Mahé and the busy narrow roads do not make it ideal for cycling.

BUDGETING FOR YOUR TRIP

Airport transfer. A taxi to Victoria should be about SCR75 (SR100 at night) and to Beau Vallon SCR400.

Buses. A ticket for any journey on Mahé or Praslin is SCR3. An all-day ticket may be purchased from bus terminals for SCR6. There are no buses on other islands.

Attractions. Nearly all nature reserves and private islands charge an entrance fee in foreign exchange, as do Marine Parks. When purchasing an excursion this is included in the price.

Car hire. A medium car hire may cost between US$ 500-700 per week. Discounts may be offered for longer periods.

Getting there. Tickets from UK cost £450–800 depending on season. Entrance fees to nature reserves and islands are included in the tour price of boat owners and tour operators.

Ferries. *Cat Cocos* fast ferry between Mahé and Praslin costs E49 on the main deck and E55 on the upper deck. The ferry between Praslin and La Digue is E14 or E17 one way.

Meals. A meal without drinks typically costs SCR100–200 per person in an inexpensive restaurant.

C

CAMPING

Camping is illegal in the Seychelles. All visitors are required to arrive at Seychelles with accommodation arranged in advance.

CAR HIRE

It is a very good idea to hire a car on Mahé as this is the best way to see the island. Car hire is less essential on Praslin, but can be economical compared to taxi fares if planning a number of outings in one day. There are no hire cars on La Digue and no roads on other islands. Cars can be delivered and returned at pre-arranged points such as the airport or your hotel.

Mini-mokes are common, but being open-sided are not ideal for locking away valuables or for staying dry in tropical downpours. Closed cars and jeeps are also readily available. Cars are delivered with sufficient petrol to get barely further than the nearest garage, so a fill-up should be the first priority. Car hire companies can tell you the location of the nearest filling station.

CLIMATE

The Seychelles is close to the equator and the climate is tropical: hot and humid all year round with low annual and daily ranges of temperature. It is dominated by two wind systems, the relatively dry southeast monsoon from May to October and the northwest monsoon which blows from November to April. Temperatures average 25–30°C (77–86°F) at sea level during the southeast monsoon and humidity is about 80 percent. Wind speeds rise at this time of year with very heavy seas around July to September. During the northwest monsoon, the wind speed and direction are less constant and temperatures are up to 3°C (5°F) higher. Heavy down-pours may occur at any time of year, particularly in the granitics. Rainfall reaches a peak around mid-December to mid-February, especially around New Year when an area of low pressure known as the Intertropical Convergence Zone, or ITCZ, passes overhead. Average monthly precipitation in the Seychelles is as the table below.

The islands lie outside the cyclone belt, though in exceptional circumstances cyclones may reach the southern islands. Between the two seasons when the sun passes vertically overhead, winds may die away completely resulting in flat calm seas and excellent water visibility but very high humidity, particularly around April. Weather forecasts can be obtained from the Met Office (tel: 4384358; www.meteo.gov.sc).

	J	F	M	A	M	J	J	A	S	O	N	D
mm	386	267	234	183	170	102	84	69	130	155	231	340
in	15.2	10.5	9.2	7.2	6.7	4.0	3.3	2.7	5.1	6.1	9.1	13.4

CLOTHING

Cool, cotton and loose is the key to comfort in the Seychelles, and high factor sun lotion is a must. Wear a T-shirt when snorkelling or swimming for any length of time. The Seychellois have learned to tolerate skimpy beachwear and topless sunbathing, but it is not appreciated around town or on public transport. Shorts are standard during the day, but many hotels and restaurants ask gentlemen to wear long trousers after 7pm. Jackets and ties are never required, even for formal business meetings. If you plan a beach-centred holiday you will need little more than a pair of flip-flops or comfortable sandals for feet, even if you plan to visit Victoria, but do not go barefoot away from the beach, as you can pick up worms this way. You may wish to pack a pair of more 'substantial' shoes for evening wear. If you plan to walk, you will need shoes, but heavy walking boots are not necessary. Trainers with a good grip and a pair of socks to protect your legs will suffice. On reefs or when landing on islands without a jetty, plastic shoes, or better still, light neoprene reef shoes are useful.

CRIME AND SAFETY

There is relatively little crime in the Seychelles, but there have been occasional incidents. Exercise common sense and do not leave bags in open cars or on beaches. Most tourists will never have a moment's concern about their personal safety or the safety of their property. Be vigilant when walking along the beach at night if there are not many people about. Do not be tempted to bring drugs into the Seychelles or try to buy them when in the country. It is taken very seriously. Once you leave the three larger islands, the risk of violence or theft is reduced to virtually nil.

For most visitors, the greatest danger is sunburn. Never underestimate the strength of the sun here, even on a cloudy day. If you expect to be in the sun for more than ten minutes you should wear high-factor lotion, and also preferably a hat. Babies should be kept out of the sun entirely. The sun reflecting off the white sand will also burn you, and the brightness can damage your eyes, so wear good-quality sunglasses.

There are dangers in the ocean that may not be obvious. Do not pick up live cone shells, which come armed with poisonous darts. Sea urchin spines can be painful and some corals can sting. Always wear shoes or flippers when visiting coral reefs. Keep to designated swimming areas and don't forget to give propellers a wide berth. On land there are no dangerous animals. The snakes are non-venomous and you would be unlikely to see one unless you go looking. The same goes for the scorpions. The palm spiders, giant millipedes, rhinoceros beetles and the cockroaches may look big and scary but are harmless. Large centipedes have a nasty bite and should be avoided. Yellow wasps have a powerful sting, but are only likely to use it if you approach their papery nests, usually hanging from tree branches. The big black wasps look fearsome but do not sting.

CUSTOMS AND ENTRY REQUIREMENTS

All nationalities need only a passport valid for at least 6 months, a local contact address and a return or onward ticket. Arrivals cards are distributed on all flights prior to landing and the tear-off portion at the bottom is stamped by Immigration and returned as a Visitor's Visa valid for 30 days. This should be retained until departure. Visas may be extended by visiting the Immigration Division (tel: 4293600), Independence House, Victoria, who will require presentation of passport, air ticket and completion of a form that requests details including evidence of sufficient funds and accommodation. A fee is payable.

The following items may be imported into the Seychelles by anyone aged 18 or over without incurring any customs duty: 400 cigarettes or 500g of tobacco; 2 litres of spirits or wine; 200ml of perfume or eau de toilette. The import of non-prescribed drugs, firearms, spear-fishing guns, plants and plant products, animals and animal products, fireworks, explosives and poisons are prohibited unless prior authorisation has been granted. Some shells (notably Triton's trumpet), unlicensed coco de mer, tortoiseshell (from hawksbill turtle), processed or live fish and live tortoises may not be exported. If buying a coco de mer, ensure it is from a licensed seller and comes with the requisite export permit.

D

DRIVING

Road conditions. Roads are fairly good, but potholes (and land slips) appear after heavy rain. Hazards are often marked by a tree branch protruding from an apparently bottomless pit. The Seychelles driving style is laid-back, and often two cars block the road while drivers wind windows down for a leisurely conversation, but at least there is little need to fear road-rage incidents. Stray cows wandering aimlessly trailing a long rope are not unusual. There is a very relaxed attitude to lane discipline. Roads are narrow, they twist and turn and have deep, unforgiving storm drains or even sheer drops down to the sea. The risk decreases dramatically on Praslin. La Digue has few vehicles and other islands do not even have roads.

Road signs. Traffic signs follow European standards.

Rules and regulations. Driving in the Seychelles is on the left. Seatbelts are compulsory (in theory at least). A valid national driving licence is required.

Speed limits. 40kph (25mph) in towns and villages, 65kph (40mph) elsewhere except on Mahé's East Coast Highway where it is 80kph (50mph).

Fuel. On Mahé, there are petrol stations near the sports complex south of Victoria, Seychelles International Airport, Beau Vallon, Mahé Beach Hotel, Anse Royale and Baie Lazare. On Praslin there are stations at Baie St Anne and Grand Anse (both 6am–8pm).

Parking. Free except in Victoria, where parking tickets can be purchased through many shops, but ample free parking near the town centre is possible by the Stadium off Francis Rachel Street. Respect double yellow lines, as police have little to do to pass the time except issue parking tickets, and tourists are not exempt.

E

ELECTRICITY

220/240V with standard 3-pin plugs as in UK, although some tourist outlets have 2-pin plugs.

EMBASSIES/CONSULATES/HIGH COMMISSIONS

There are few diplomatic missions in the Seychelles and there is no representation for Australia, Ireland, Canada and South Africa.

France (Embassy): La Ciotat a Mont Fleuri, Victoria, Mahé, tel: 4382500.
UK (High Commission): Oliaji Trade Centre, Francis Rachel Street, Victoria, Mahé, tel: 4283666.
US (Consulate): Oliaji Trade Centre, Francis Rachel Street, Victoria, Mahé, tel: 4225256.

EMERGENCIES
Dial **999** for police, fire brigade or ambulance services.

G

GAY AND LESBIAN TRAVELLERS
There is no gay night scene in the Seychelles, although there are certainly gay Seychellois. Although you are unlikely to be subjected to violence, this is a mostly traditional Catholic country and some Seychellois would be offended by any ostentatious displays of affection between same-sex couples. Discretion is advised, but there is no need to be particularly afraid of abuse.

GETTING THERE
From the UK. Air Seychelles www.airseychelles.com flies nonstop from Heathrow and Paris. Emirates www.emirates.com has connections several times per week via Dubai from London, Manchester, Birmingham and Glasgow. Qatar Airways www.qatarairways.com has connections several times per week from London and Manchester. Kenya Airways has connections from London via Nairobi.

Some UK-based agents specialise in holidays to the Seychelles and often offer good deals on their websites. In particular, these include: Just Seychelles (tel: 01342547001) and Seychelles Travel (tel: 01202 877 330, www.seychelles-travel.co.uk).
From outside Europe. In addition to the connections via Europe, Qatar, Dubai and Kenya, Air Seychelles has flights from Singapore and Johannesburg.

GUIDED WALKS

Guided walks are an excellent way to see native flora and fauna that you might otherwise miss, and to learn about local culture, from the use of spices and medicinal plants to the making of *baka*. On Mahé, local naturalist Basil Beaudouin (tel: 4241790) leads walks from 1–2 hours up to a full day of 6–8 hours; he is available to talk about his walks at the Coral Strand Hotel, average price SCR 350 per person.

On Praslin, Bois Mare Nature Guide, Cap Samy (tel: 2513370) offers a variety of walks. Coco de Mer Hotel (tel: 4290555) offers guided walks of the nearby Jean Baptiste Nature Trail.

H

HEALTH AND MEDICAL CARE

Standards of health and hygiene in the Seychelles are high. There is neither malaria nor yellow fever. A yellow fever vaccination certificate is required by all travellers aged over one year arriving from infected areas or who have passed through areas where it is partly or wholly endemic, within the preceding six days. There are very occasional outbreaks of dengue fever, but the risk is very slight. In 2006, an outbreak of chikungunya, also borne by mosquitoes, affected many people in the islands of the western Indian Ocean including the Seychelles.

Behram's Pharmacy (tel: 4225559), Victoria House, Victoria has basic non-prescription medical supplies, but does not stock a wide range. Any medicines you may need are best brought with you and certainly anything of a specialist nature.

Mains water is normally chlorinated and, whilst quite safe, may have a slightly unpleasant taste. Bottled water is available. Local meat, poultry, seafood, fruit and vegetables (the latter after washing) are safe to eat.

There is a large general hospital in Victoria (tel: 388020) and hospitals at Anse Royale (tel: 4371222), Baie St Anne (tel: 4232333) on Praslin and Logan (tel: 4234255) on La Digue. In addition, there are clinics in every village of any size, but medical facilities are limited. Visitors may obtain emergency treatment for a basic consultancy fee. There are private doctors in and around Victoria, including Dr Jivan (tel: 4324008) and Le Chantier Health Services (tel: 4324008).

I am not well. **Mon pa byen.**
Call an ambulance. **Apellanbilans.**
We need a doctor. **Nou bezwen en dokter.**
They've had an accident. **Zot in ganny en aksidan.**
Where is the nearest clinic? **Kote klinik pli pre silvouple?**

HOLIDAYS

The following are official public holidays. If a public holiday falls on a Sunday, the Monday automatically becomes a holiday. Most of the tourist attractions remain open on public holidays except on 1 January, but all offices and some restaurants close. Supermarkets are closed but many small village shops will remain open.

1–2 January New Year
1 May Labour Day
5 June Liberation Day (Anniversary of 1977 Coup)
18 June National Day
29 June Independence Day
15 August Assumption/La Digue Festival
1 November All Saints' Day
8 December Immaculate Conception
25 December Christmas Day
Moveable dates:
Late March/April Good Friday
Late March/April Easter Monday
Mid-June Corpus Christi

L

LANGUAGE

There are three national languages: English, French and Creole. On all the islands most tourists will visit, you will get by easily in English or basic French, and many Seychellois, particularly those in the tourism industry, also speak a little Italian or German. Creole is derived from simplified French, but readily adapts words and phrases from various sources, especially modern English. It is not unusual to hear Seychellois drifting without a thought from Creole into English. You may find that older people, or workers on the remoter islands, are more comfortable in Creole, but nearly everyone will understand you if you stick to simple words in French or English. Creole is not pronounced with a French accent. There is no need to practise Creole at hotels or with tour operators, who will be entirely fluent in English.

> please **silvouple**
> thank you **mersi**
> How are you? **Ki dir?**
> I'm fine, thank you. **Mon byen mersi.**
> I don't understand. **Mon pa konpran.**
> Do you speak English? **Ou kapab koz angle?**
> Please speak more slowly. **Koze pli lantman silvouple.**

M

MAPS

Bookshops sell good maps of the main islands. In addition, excellent detailed large-scale maps of all islands can be purchased from the Land and Survey Division, Ground Floor, Independence House, 5th June Avenue, Victoria.

MEDIA

Few international magazines are available, though *Newsweek* and *Time* are often available at some bookshops, especially at the airport. The British High Commission in Victoria provides British newspapers for reading in the reception area, usually somewhat out of date.

The *Seychelles Nation* is a Government-owned newspaper, which appears daily except Sunday. It tends to give a rather rosy view of political affairs and the local economy. *Regar* and *Seychelles Weekly* are run by opposition political parties and offer an alternative view including many stories that never appear in the Government-controlled press.

Most larger hotels have televisions with a few satellite or cable channels, typically including CNN, Discovery Channel, sports channels and a French channel or two.

BBC World Service have a relay station on Mahé but this beams directly across the sea to Africa. There is good reception on 106.2 medium wave in and around Victoria, but this peters out at Machabee in the north, and south of the airport. Reception is only possible on FM elsewhere, but is reasonably good.

MONEY

Currency. The Seychelles rupee is divided into 100 cents. Bank notes are available in denominations of 500, 100, 50, 25 and 10. Coins are in denominations of SCR5 and 1, and 25, 10 and 5 cents.

Currency exchange. Banks give better exchange rates than hotels. Exchange facilities are available at the airport, in Victoria and in larger villages. Keep currency exchange receipts to facilitate re-exchange on departure. You may not need to change very much money into rupees as many costs, including excursions, car hire, hotel bills and island entrance fees, are fixed by law in foreign exchange (usually Euros). Even the airport's duty-free shop only accepts foreign currency.

Credit and debit cards. Major international credit cards are widely accepted. American Express and Diners Club are less popular than Visa and Mastercard. Credit and debit cards are useful for getting cash from ATMs at banks, especially outside banking hours. There are often long queues at the tills during banking hours in Victoria, especially at the end of the month.

Travellers cheques. Accepted in most hotels, guesthouses, restaurants and shops. Banks will give a better rate of exchange. Sterling and US dollars are fine, but many hotel rates and entrance fees are fixed in Euros.

The Black Market. It is illegal to exchange foreign currency with anyone other than an authorised bank or tourism outlet. However, many visitors are approached at some point and offered a considerably better rate than that legally available. Some taxis and shops may offer favourable rates for payment in foreign currency. Government attempts to control this were strong at one time but have now relaxed, and transactions take place surprisingly openly.

Where can I find a bank? **Kote labank?**
I'm just looking. **Mon pe rode selman.**
Do you accept credit cards? **Eski ou pran kart kredi?**
How much is it? **Konbyen sa?**
It's too expensive. **I tro ser.**
Have you got...? **Eski ou annan...?**
I'll take this one. **Mon pran sa enn.**

O

OPENING TIMES

Office hours are 8am–4pm with an hour for lunch, noon–1pm. Most shops open Mon–Fri 8.30am–5pm, Sat 8.30am–noon, with many smaller stores opening longer hours and at weekends. Some shops will close their grill doors after a certain hour at night (to deter drunks) and serve you through the bars. Tourist attractions are generally open daily, but some islands only on certain days. Most restaurants serve lunch noon–2pm. Some open for dinner only, which usually commences about 7pm. A few restaurants close on Sundays and public holidays.

P

POLICE

Seychelles police are very friendly and responsive to tourists, if not particularly swift or efficient. Dial 999 for emergencies. For Central Police Station Victoria, call 4288000. At Beau Vallon call 4247242. On Praslin call 4233251 and on La Digue 4234251.

POST OFFICE

The main post office is in Victoria next to the clock tower on Independence Avenue (Mon–Fri 8.30am–4pm, Sat 8.30am–noon). There are sub post offices at Grande Anse, Praslin and La Passe, La Digue. Public post boxes are available outside most police stations. Hotels sell stamps and will post mail.

PUBLIC TRANSPORT

Air. Air Seychelles (tel: 4 391000) operates 20 or more flights daily between Mahé and Praslin throughout the day. Scheduled flights are also operated to Bird, Denis and Frégate. Islands Development Company (tel: 4384640) operates planes to Alphonse and Desroches resorts and charters to other outer islands where there are airstrips.

Bus. Buses are cheap and of a fairly good standard. Routes and timetables are geared to local requirements and you may have a long wait at bus stops outside normal working hours. There are fewer buses on Praslin. On La Digue, open-sided lorries (camions) are also available from Chez Michelin, La Passe (tel: 4234304).

Ferry. The fast ferry *Cat Cocos* operates twice daily between the Inter-Island Quay, Victoria and Baie St Anne, Praslin, taking one hour each way. It has a Club Class upper deck for 34 passengers and a main cabin for 125. Advance booking is advisable especially at weekends (tel: Mahé 4324843). Local schooners carry mainly cargo, but will also take passengers, the journey lasting three hours. Ferries are the main form of transport between Praslin and La Digue, run by Inter-island Ferry Pty. Ltd (tel: 4232329/232394). There are seven return journeys Mon–Sat from 7am–5.15pm from Praslin and 7.30am–5.45pm from La Digue. On Sundays, there is an extra round trip with the last ferry from Praslin at 5.45pm and from La Digue at 6.15pm. It is essential to book in advance. Arrive 15 minutes before departure of all ferries.

Helicopter. Helicopter Seychelles (tel: 4385858) operates a shuttle service between Mahé, Praslin and La Digue. Transfers by helicopter are available to Plantation Club, Mahé and Lemuria Resort, Praslin and to island resorts at Bird, Cousine, Denis, Félicité, Frégate, North, Silhouette and St Anne. Day trips to Aride and other islands can be arranged.

Taxi. Taxis are supposed to be metered, but in practice most drivers claim the meter is not working. It is then best to fix the fare in advance to avoid arguments. There are plenty of taxis available on Mahé at the airport and Victoria at Albert Street taxi rank and on Independence Avenue.

On Praslin taxis are available at the airport, Baie St Anne jetty and elsewhere. There is only four one motorised taxi on La Digue and it is sensible to book it in advance if you have heavy cases or a deadline (tel: 2582725); alternatively, ox-carts still provide a slightly slower, bumpier service.

R

RELIGION

Eighty-seven percent of Seychellois are Catholics, but the Anglican Church, Seventh Day Adventists and others are also represented. There is one mosque and one Hindu temple in Victoria. There are Catholic and Anglican cathedrals in Victoria, and there are many Catholic parish churches in the villages where visitors are welcome but should dress fairly smartly.

T

TELEPHONE

Seychelles country code is 248. There are no area codes within the Seychelles, where all telephone numbers (including mobiles) have seven digits.

You can make direct-dial local and international calls from public phone boxes, which take coins or cards (obtainable from many shops). Calls can also be made and cards purchased at the offices of the two companies offering local services, Airtel (tel: 4600600), Providence, Mahé and Cable & Wireless (tel: 4284000), Francis Rachel Street, Victoria, Mahé. To make an international call dial 00, followed by the country code then the number omitting the initial 0. Hotels have a high mark-up on calls from rooms.

If you use a computer to make international calls using services such as Skype, the reception to and from the Seychelles is very good.

TIME ZONES

Seychelles time is GMT plus 4 hours or BST plus 3 hours.

New York	London	Seychelles	Sydney	Auckland
3am	8am	noon	5pm	7pm

TIPPING

Tipping is not a big feature, but it is certainly appreciated when you feel it is merited and in restaurants where a service charge is not specifically mentioned on the menu. Taxi drivers whose meters are not working will probably have included their own tip calculation in the fare they quote.

TOILETS

On the whole it would be prudent to make use of your hotel facilities before you leave. There are public toilets behind the beach at Beau Vallon, in the Botanical Gardens, at airports on Mahé and Praslin and at Baie St Anne jetty, Praslin. You may make use of the toilets at the café or restaurant where you have your lunch or dinner and at the Pirates' Arms in Independence Avenue, which is open all day and at nights. Islands open for day visits sometimes have toilets of the deep-drop variety, which are fine once you get used to the idea. In Victoria, there are public facilities at Victoria Taxi Rank.

TOURIST INFORMATION

Tourist Offices Abroad

South Africa: 402 Bree Castle House, 68 Bree Street, Capetown; tel: +27 214260104

UK: 130-132 Buckingham Palace Road, London SW1W9SA; tel: +44 (0) 2072456106 (serves UK, Ireland, Netherlands, Sweden, Denmark, Finland and Norway).

Tourist Offices in the Seychelles

Seychelles Tourist Board is based at Bel Ombre, Mahé, but also operates outlets in key centres for tourists where brochures, maps and general advice are available.

Mahé: Independence House, Victoria (Mon–Fri 8am–5pm, Sat 9am–noon; tel: 4610800).

Praslin: Praslin Airport, Amitie and Baie St Anne jetty (Mon–Fri 8am–1pm, 2–4pm, Sat and Public Holidays 8am–noon, Sun closed; tel: 4233346).

La Digue: La Passe (Mon–Fri 8am–4.30pm, Sat 9am–noon, 3–4.30pm, Sun 8am–noon; tel: 4234393).

W

WEBSITES AND INTERNET CAFES

Useful websites for planning your trip:

www.airseychelles.com Air Seychelles Flights and general information.

www.shta.sc Seychelles Hospitality & Tourism Association.

www.aspureasitgets.com Seychelles Tourist Board general information.

www.seychelles.travel General information.

Internet cafés are can be found all over. In Victoria, they include Atlas (tel: 304060), Trinity House, Albert Street; Digitech Internet (tel: 225521), Salamat House, La Poudriere Lane; Double Click (tel: 610590), Maison La Rosiere, and Kokonet (tel: 322000), Pirates Arms Arcade. On Praslin there is Grand Anse Internet Café (tel: 712073), 50m (55yds) from the petrol station. On La Digue, there are three bureaux within a short distance of the jetty at La Passe. These are Safari Club Internet Bureau near the Post Office, Cybercafe next to Tarosa Restaurant and La Digue Internet Café just round the first left turning south of the jetty.

WEIGHTS AND MEASURES

The metric system is in common use, but the imperial system is still widely understood.

Y

YOUTH HOSTELS

There are no youth hostels in the Seychelles.

RECOMMENDED HOTELS

The Seychelles offers the full range of accommodation from self-catering apartments to luxury hotels. Hotels come well up to international standards and many are equipped with air conditioning (or, at the very least, ceiling fans), private bathrooms, swimming pools, watersports and other sporting facilities. There are no high-rise hotels and the vast majority are built on just one or two levels.

Website addresses are only given where these are specific to the hotel. There is a 15 percent Value Added Tax which should be included in quotations. Prices are generally high by international standards, but this is not a mass-market destination and there has been a deliberate move by the Government towards high-return but relatively low-volume tourism. The following guide indicates prices for a double room in high season (prices should be used as an approximate guide only):

€€€€	over 350 euros
€€€	250–350 euros
€€	150–250 euros
€	below 150 euros

MAHÉ

Anse Soleil Beachcomber €€ *Anse Soleil, tel: 4361461, fax: 4361460,* www.ansesoleilbeachcomber.com. A small hotel with five standard and five superior rooms, all with veranda and a beautiful sea view of one of the most exquisite beaches, with excellent swimming and snorkelling.

Banyan Tree Seychelles €€€€ *Anse Intendance, tel: 4383500/383555, fax: 4383600,* www.banyantree.com/seychelles. Forty-seven very private, spacious pool villas situated on wild Intendance Bay, one of the world's most beautiful beaches, all rooms with spectacular views.

Beau Vallon Bungalows € *Beau Vallon, tel: 4247382/514382, mobile: 2515 025,* www.beauvallon-bungallows.com. Twelve comfortable self-catering bungalows close to Beau Vallon beach and to several excellent restaurants.

Berjaya Beau Vallon Bay Beach Resort & Casino €€€ *Beau Vallon, tel: 4287287, fax: 4 247943,* www.berjayahotel.com. A large hotel with all rooms air-conditioned. Excellent watersports, sports and diving facilities, a casino and a choice of bars and restaurants including Japanese, Chinese and a pizzeria.

Berjaya Mahé Beach Resort €€ *Port Glaud, tel: 4385385, fax: 4378117.* A large hotel on the otherwise quiet west coast of Mahé. Large attractive grounds, two restaurants. Complimentary shuttle-bus service to Victoria and Beau Vallon.

Chalets d'Anse Forbans €€ *Anse Forbans, tel: 4366111, fax: 4366161,* www.forbans.com. Fourteen comfortable fully equipped self-catering bungalows at reasonable prices, located on the beach in the quiet south of Mahé. Upon arrival, guests are given some basic groceries, a beach towel and snorkelling equipment.

Coco d'Or Hotel €€ *Beau Vallon, tel: 4247331, fax: 4247454;* www.cocodor.sc. This hotel has twenty-four standard and three deluxe rooms with balcony or terrace, satellite TV, air-conditioning and en suite. Beau Vallon Bay is just a few minutes' walk. There is a Chinese restaurant, a pizzeria and a main restaurant, and snacks can be served at the pool.

Coral Strand Hotel €€ *Beau Vallon, tel: 4291000, fax: 4291000;* www.coralstrand.com. A large, friendly hotel right on Beau Vallon Beach with several restaurants including the best Indian restaurant and a popular pool bar. Watersports and dive facilities are second to none. Glass-bottom boat and game fishing are also available.

Les Pieds dans L'eau Holiday Apartments €€ *East Coast Road, Anse Royale Village, tel: 4430 100.* Apartments with stunning panoramic views are right on the beach at Anse Royale offering safe swimming and great snorkelling spots. Their restaurant serves good quality local and international dishes.

Hotel Bel Air €€ *Bel Air, tel: 4224416,* www.seychelles.net/belair. With just seven rooms, this is more a guesthouse than a hotel. It is conveniently located on the hillside above Victoria, good for visitors on business.

La Résidence € *Anse La Mouche, tel: mobile 4271733, 4410529, www.laresidence.sc*. Self-catering apartments with 5 studios and 3 villas. Situated 50m (160ft) above the beautiful bay of Anse la Mouche on Mahé's unspoilt west coast.

Avani Seychelles Barbarons Resort and Spa €€€ *Barbarons Beach, tel: 4673000, www.minorhotels.com*. The only hotel on this lovely beach, with restaurant and bar overlooking the view. It is also within walking distance of an excellent trail (Sentier Vacoa Trail) that leads into the hills. Facilities include tennis, swimming pool, watersports, mini-golf and snorkelling. Diving is contracted to a padi centre 15 minutes away (transport provided free).

Le Méridien Fisherman's Cove €€€€ *Beau Vallon, tel: 4677000, www.starwoodhotels.com*. A large five-star hotel, with all 70 rooms facing the quiet southern corner of Beau Vallon beach. Facilities include a fitness centre and spa, tennis, and free non-motorised watersports.

Le Petit Village €€€ *Bel Ombre, tel: 4284969, fax: 4247771*. Upmarket self-catering in 12 distinctive log-cabin style studio or two-bedroom apartments within close proximity of all the facilities of Beau Vallon. All rooms are serviced daily.

Hilton Seychelles Northholme Resort & Spa €€€€ *Glacis, tel: 4299000, fax: 4299004, www3.hilton.com*. 15 luxurious villas on a hillside overlooking Silhouette and North Island, with a small private cove. Only children age 13 and over are accepted in order to maintain the serenity of the resort. Infinity pools blend with the view of the Indian Ocean out to Silhouette and North islands. Complimentary services include transport to nearby watersports and dive centres.

Panorama €-€€ *Beau Vallon, tel: 4247300, fax: 4247947*. Ten double rooms in this small, well-established family-run hotel. Excellent location directly overlooking the beautiful Beau Vallon beach. Good snorkelling is available at the northern end of the beach.

Kempinski Seychelles Resort €€€-€€€€ *Baie Lazare, tel: 4386666, fax: 4386699, www.kempinskiu.com*. A large hotel with 200 spacious rooms situated on a long sandy beach in the secluded southwestern corner of Mahé. Excellent facilities from land and watersports to casino and a large swimming pool. Beautiful grounds in a former coconut plantation including an attractive lakeside.

Sun Properties & Resort €€ *Beau Vallon, tel: 4285555, fax: 4247224.* Twenty well-equipped rooms around a swimming pool, this is the best possible compromise between self-catering and an inclusive resort, with both in-house restaurant and nearby facilities of Coral Strand, Coco d-Or and Beau Vallon restaurants. Just a short stroll to the beach, watersports and diving services.

Sunset Beach Resort €€€€ *Glacis, tel: 4261111, fax: 4261221,* www. thesunsethotelgroup.com. An attractive hotel on the northwest coast with a beautiful bar area situated on a promontory by the sea and adjacent to an excellent beach, good for snorkelling. No children under 10 years old are allowed. Watersports and diving can be arranged at Beau Vallon.

Wharf Hotel & Marina €€€ *Providence, tel: 4670700, fax: 4601701,* www.wharfseychelles.com. Between the airport and Victoria, this small luxury hotel is ideal for short stays on Mahé before flying out or joining a cruise. Fifteen luxury rooms plus one 4-room penthouse. Facilities include an excellent restaurant, swimming pool, massage facilities and berths for up to 60 yachts.

Xanadu Chalets €€ *Anse Cachee, tel: 4366522, fax: 4366344.* These eight large luxurious one- or two-bedroom chalets are located at the remote southernmost end of the island, on a gentle hillside above the ocean and a private beach. A hire car is recommended for this out-of-the-way location, ideal for a quiet, relaxing and private getaway.

PRASLIN

Berjaya Praslin Beach Hotel €€ *Anse Volbert, tel: 4286286, fax: 4232244,* www.berjayahotel.com/praslin. A fairly large hotel (79 rooms and suites) with good facilities at Anse Volbert next to Côte d'Or. Non-motorised watersports are free to guests. The hotel offers daily theme evenings with local bands. Nature walks with a guide are also offered, as well as trips to one of the world's finest beaches, Anse Lazio.

Britannia Hotel € *Grand Anse, tel: 4233215*, www.britanniapraslin.com. A small, cosy, comfortable hotel with a big swimming pool situated in a tropical garden visited by black parrots. A quiet inland location off the main road but only 5 minutes from the beach. Excellent restaurant serves Creole and international cuisine.

Chateau de Feuilles Hotel €€€€ *Pointe Cabris Estate, Baie Ste Anne, tel: 4290000, fax: 4290029*, www.chateau-seychelles.com. This is a small, luxurious hotel, with just 9 rooms on a small estate located on a headland above Baie Ste Anne with spectacular views over the islands. A free rental car is allocated to each room. At the weekend, there are free and exclusive excursions to Grand Soeur. The restaurant's inventive cuisine specialises in seafood and fish.

Coco de Mer Hotel & Black Parrot Suites €€€ *Anse Bois de Rose, tel: 4290555, fax: 4290440*, www.cocodemer.com. Situated on the peaceful southwest coast. There are 52 spacious rooms and suites, all with private verandas facing the sea and the setting sun. Facilities here include watersports and mini golf. Bicycles and snorkelling equipment are both available for a nominal charge. Deep-sea fishing and excursions to nearby islands can be arranged.

Hirondelle Guest House € *Côte d'Or, tel/fax: 4232243*, www.hirondelle-seychelles.com. Hirondelle faces one of the most beautiful beaches on Praslin, Anse Volbert. One three-bedroom house and four self-catering apartments, in close proximity to all the restaurants and watersports facilities of Côte d'Or.

Indian Ocean Lodge €€-€€€ *Grand Anse, tel: 4283838*, www.indianoceanlodge.com. A medium-sized hotel (32 rooms in eight units) on the long expanse of Grand Anse beach. Daily excursions by boat can be arranged to one of the nature reserve islands of Aride, Curieuse or Cousin. Live music is provided some nights, or, if that is not enough, the Jungle Disco is not far away. A free daily shuttle service to Côte d'Or is provided.

La Cuvette Hotel € *Grand Anse, tel: 4233005, fax: 4233960*. A small, cheerful, eight-room hotel with a courtyard and small swimming pool. Situated on a quiet road lined by mango and breadfruit trees, just a few minutes from the beach. Cosy dining room offers excellent Creole cuisine.

L'Archipel Hotel & Restaurant €€€€ *Anse Gouvernement, tel: 4284700, mob. 4321293,* www.larchipel.com. A first-rate medium-sized upmarket hotel (30 rooms) in a secluded sheltered cove. Complimentary snorkelling, windsurfing and canoeing equipment are offered, and other watersports facilities are available at nearby Côte d'Or. The restaurant is excellent, and candlelit dinner dances are organised twice a week.

Le Domaine de La Reserve Hotel & Restaurant €€€ *Anse Petit Cour, tel: 4298000, fax: 4232166,* www.domainedelareserve.sc. A charismatic, charming hotel on a secluded quiet beach, not far from all the watersports opportunities of Côte d'Or.

La Vanille Bungalows & Restaurant *Anse La Blague, tel: 4232178, fax: 4232284.* A small six-room hotel (4 standard rooms & 2 superior rooms) built among the rocks away from the main tourist centres on the wild coast of Anse la Blague. Features a very nice beach-side restaurant.

Le Duc de Praslin €€ *Anse Volbert, tel: 4294800, email:* leduc@seychelles.net, www.leduc-seychelles.com. A cheerful 18-room hotel in a lovely setting, which includes an orchid garden with more than 100 varieties, and a lovely fish pond. The restaurant serves excellent Creole cuisine. Close to all the watersports facilities of Côte d'Or.

Le Laurier Eco Hotel and Restaurant € *Côte d'Or, tel: 4232241, email:* laurier@seychelles.net, www.laurier-seychelles.com. Quaint, inexpensive guesthouse with four rooms, three minutes by foot to the beach. Also a good restaurant with Creole buffet and barbecue. Babysitting services can be provided on request.

Constance Lemuria Resort €€€€ *Anse Kerlan, tel: 4281281, fax: 4281001;* www.constancehotels.com. Frequently hailed as one of the best hotels in the world, facilities include the only 18-hole golf course in the Seychelles, business centre, Jacuzzis, sauna, children's club, diving and watersports. The grounds embrace three beaches, including Anse Georgette, one of the world's best. Accommodation includes 96 suites, eight villas and, for those who can afford it, a rather special Presidential Suite.

Marechiaro Hotel €€€ *Grand Anse, tel: 4283888, fax: 4233993.* Twenty-five well-furnished timber and granite rooms situated on the beach. Watersports facilities and tennis are available, and a PADI dive centre is situated nearby. The excellent Capri Restaurant specialises in Italian and Creole cuisine.

Paradise Sun Resort €€€€ *Côte d'Or, tel: reservations +27 11 461 9744,* www.tsogosun.com. A large hotel with excellent views of Côte d'Or and Curieuse Marine National Park. Complimentary kayaks, windsurfers and snorkelling equipment are available. Evenings often feature traditional music, including *moutya* evenings against the backdrop of a beach fire.

Villa Flamboyant €€ *Anse St Sauveur, tel/fax: 4233036.* This is a lovely little guesthouse on a secluded beach with a lovely woodland garden of fruit trees, flame trees and others visited by black parrots. Ideal if you are looking for a peaceful vacation in a friendly-family atmosphere.

Villas de Mer €€ *Grand Anse, tel: 4233972, fax: 4233015,* www.seychelles-resa.com. Situated on the west coast of Praslin near the airport. Very nice, simple facilities on Grand Anse beach. Ten spacious mini-suite bedrooms (most accommodate up to two adults and two children) in three bungalows and a main plantation-style house. Deep-sea fishing, diving and excursions can be arranged upon request.

LA DIGUE

Bernique €€ *La Passe, tel: 4234229, mobile 2 514203;* www.berniqueguesthouse-seychelles.com. Twelve rooms and a Creole restaurant situated in the interior of La Digue, 5 minutes by bicycle from the jetty and the beach. Run by one of the veteran singers and entertainers of La Digue, with a welcoming atmosphere.

Chateau St Cloud €€ *Anse Reunion, tel: 4234346, fax: 4234545;* www.chateau-stcloud.com. Situated inland at the foot of the mountain, this is a very untypical, informal and charming hotel. The main building is a reminder of the great wealth that vanilla production brought to La Digue in the colonial past. Excellent Creole food is served in the restaurant.

Choppy's Beach Bungalow Bar & Restaurant €€ *La Passe, tel: 4234224, fax: 4234088.* Two bungalows each with two rooms plus six separate rooms and an attractive beach bar and restaurant. Local bands sometimes provide entertainment.

Hotel L'Ocean €€ *Anse Severe, tel: 4234180, fax: 4234308,* www.hotel ocean.info. The hotel commands the northern tip of La Digue, with superb views of Félicité and The Sisters from the verandas of each of the eight rooms. Sometimes turtles or dolphins can be spotted from the hotel terrace. This is not far from La Passe but is still a peaceful corner of the island.

La Digue Island Lodge €€€€ *Anse Reunion, tel: 4234233, fax: 4234100,* www.ladigue.sc. The largest and most famous hotel on La Digue. The 69 rooms range from steep-sided A-frame chalets constructed with takamaka wood and latanier thatching to the attractive if slightly whacky Yellow House, an old colonial house with 9 rooms. Free excursions to neighbouring islands and tickets to L'Union Estate are provided to guests.

Paradise Flycatcher €€ *L'Union, tel: 4234422, fax: 4234423.* Self-catering but with a restaurant featuring Creole cuisine. Inland, just a few minutes from the beach in a peaceful garden, this consists of four chalets each with two large bedrooms. The ideal accommodation for families or a group of friends on a budget.

Patatran Village €€ *Anse Patates, tel: 4294300, fax: 4294390,* www. patatranseychelles.com. With twelve bungalows (four for families), the hotel is perched on a headland with beautiful views.

Vanilla Guest House € *La Passe, tel: 2587715, fax: 4234289.* Offers four rooms on the beach front within walking distance of the jetty. Fairly basic, without air-conditioning, but roomy, clean and pleasant.

Villa Authentique € *La Passe, tel/fax: 4234413.* Six air-conditioned rooms, two of which are self-catering, two minutes from the beach. Very friendly family atmosphere.

Alphonse Island Resort €€€ *tel: 27 21 556 5763,* www.alphonse-island.com. The most remote and perhaps most beautiful coral island, 400km (250 miles) and a one-hour flight southwest of Mahé. Twenty-five spacious thatched chalets and five executive villas all with air-conditioning, veranda and Jacuzzi. Excellent diving and fly-fishing opportunities, plus visits to nearby Bijoutier and St Francois. Perfect for a relaxing, luxurious getaway.

Anonyme Resort €€€ *tel: 4380100/710111, fax: 4380101.* A small resort of just seven luxury villas off the east coast of Mahé. Anonyme is an 'outer island' experience within sight of the International Airport. When leaving, you even go direct to airport check-in by boat. Excellent restaurant with flexible meal times to suit you. Watersports facilities are available.

Bird Island Lodge €€ *tel: 4224925 (Victoria Head Office), 4323322 (Lodge), fax: 4225074,* www.birdislandseychelles.com. Simplicity is the theme at this get-away-from-it-all island. Rooms are spacious with ceiling fans, but no TV, telephone or radio disturbs the tranquillity. Excellent cuisine and a family atmosphere. Guided nature walks, deep-sea fishing, nesting turtles, a huge tern colony from Apr–Oct and rare migrants (mainly Oct–Dec) are among the attractions.

Cousine Island Resort €€€€ *tel: 27 117063 104, fax: 27 117064 752,* www.cousineisland.com. A maximum of ten guests share a private nature reserve with giant tortoises, turtles and thousands of seabirds. Some 3,500 indigenous trees have been planted since 1992 to make this one of the few islands returned to nature since the days when coconut plantations ruled supreme.

Denis Private Island €€€€ *tel: 4288963, 4295999, fax: 4321010,* www.denisisland.com. Twenty-five large, luxurious rooms. A wonderful island retreat, perched on the edge of the Seychelles plateau where the ocean floor plunges to huge depths. Fishing and watersports are good year-round. Several nature trails criss-cross the island, where endemic land birds are to be seen.

Desroches Island   €€€€ *tel: 27 82496 4570,* www.desrochesvilla
sales.com. At 250km (156 miles) or 35 minutes' flight from Mahé,
this is the closest island of the Amirantes and the largest of the
group. Excellent beaches for swimming or watersports, and excellent diving during the calmer months.

Félicité €€€€ *tel: 4292525, fax: 4234132,* www.ladigue.sc. A small
private lodge for up to 16 guests, who rent their own private island.
Excellent service, cuisine and swimming on La Pernice beach. Associated with La Digue Island Lodge, whose extensive facilities are
available to guests.

Frégate Island Private €€€€ *tel: 07 22 19 008 071, email:* welcome@
fregate.com, www.fregate.com. A luxury hideaway with 16 villas. Excellent beaches and nature trails, which can be explored by mountain
bike if walking gets too much. Children are welcome. The 11-metre
(37-ft) *Little Frégate Bird* is available for fishing trips and the 13-metre
(43-ft) *Frégate Bird* is available for charter. Helicopter trips to Lemuria
Golf Course can be arranged.

Hilton Seychelles Labriz Resort and Spa, Silhouette Island €€€ *tel:
429 3949, fax: 429 3939,* www3.hilton.com. Luxurious villas of vary-
ing style nestling between the beautiful beach of Anse La Passe and
the towering mountain peaks, 45 minutes by boat or 15 minutes by
helicopter from Mahé. Amenities include an excellent spa, several
restaurants, diving, watersports and nature walks on this large but
sparsely populated island.

North Island €€€€ *tel: 4293100, fax: 4293150,* www.north-island.
com. Eleven large private villas on an island with a heavy emphasis
on conservation and nature trails to be explored. The hotel has been
constructed largely from materials reaped from the rehabilitation
process. The adjacent waters are excellent for game fishing, snorkelling and diving (all these facilities are provided).

INDEX

Berlitz POCKET GUIDE

SEYCHELLES

Second Edition 2017

Editor: Kate Drynan
Author: Adrian Skerrett
Head of Production: Rebeka Davies
Picture Editor: Tom Smyth
Cartography Update: Carte
Update Production: AM Services
Photography Credits: Alamy 6TL, 40, 55, 73;
AWL Images 4ML, 29; Berjaya Hotels & Resorts
97; Corbis 71; Denis Island Resort 5MC, 78;
Frégate Island 74/75; Getty Images 4MC, 5MC,
5M, 6TL, 7T, 8R, 9, 12, 15, 19, 22, 24, 30, 34, 35,
41, 42, 47, 50, 56, 57, 59, 60, 62, 63, 64, 65, 67,
69, 70, 72, 76, 80, 81, 84, 91, 92, 95, 101, 102,
104, 105, 106, 108; iStock 4TL, 5M, 7T, 8L, 10, 31,
94, 98; Joe Laurence/Seychelles News Agency
7TC; Leonardo 37; National Maritime Museum
17; New Mauritius Hotels Ltd 49; Public domain
20, 21; Shutterstock 4TC, 5TC, 7M, 9R, 27, 32/33,
46, 53, 68, 83, 87, 93; SuperStock 5T, 6ML, 39,
44, 88, 89
Cover Picture: Shutterstock

Distribution
UK, Ireland and Europe: Apa Publications
(UK) Ltd; sales@insightguides.com
United States and Canada: Ingram Publisher
Services; ips@ingramcontent.com
Australia and New Zealand: Woodslane;
info@woodslane.com.au
Southeast Asia: Apa Publications (SN) Pte;
singaporeoffice@insightguides.com
Hong Kong, Taiwan and China:
Apa Publications (HK) Ltd;

hongkongoffice@insightguides.com
Worldwide: Apa Publications (UK) Ltd;
sales@insightguides.com

**Special Sales, Content Licensing
and CoPublishing**
Insight Guides can be purchased in bulk
quantities at discounted prices. We can create
special editions, personalised jackets and
corporate imprints tailored to your needs.
sales@insightguides.com;
www.insightguides.biz

Contact us
Every effort has been made to provide accurate
information in this publication, but changes are
inevitable. The publisher cannot be responsible
for any resulting loss, inconvenience or injury.
We would appreciate it if readers would call our
attention to any errors or outdated information.
We also welcome your suggestions; please
contact us at: berlitz@apaguide.co.uk
www.insightguides.com/berlitz

Berlitz®

speaking your language

phrase book & dictionary
phrase book & CD

Available in: Arabic, Brazilian
Chinese, Croatian, Czech*, Danish
German, Greek, Hebrew*, Hindi*
Korean, Latin American Spanish,
Norwegian, Polish, Portuguese,
Turkish, Vietnamese
*Book only

www.berlitzpublishing.com